The England of Henry Taunt

Victorian Photographer

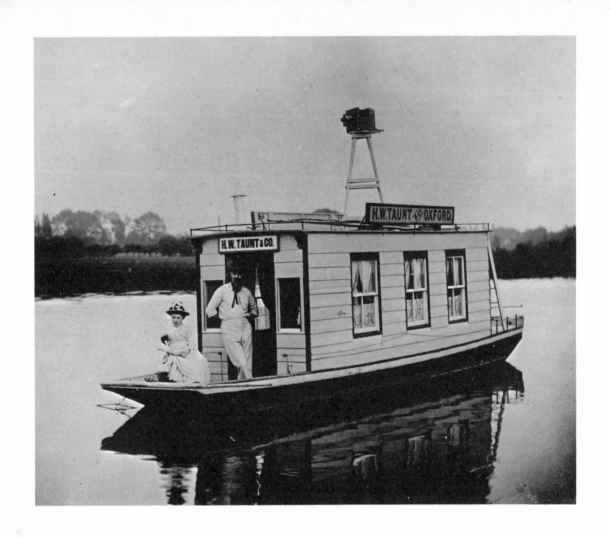

Henry W. Taunt aboard his boat on the river at Oxford in the 1880s, with his camera mounted aloft, from which vantage point he often photographed the University boating events.

The England of Henry Taunt

Victorian Photographer

his Thames. his Oxford. his Home Counties and Travels
his Portraits. Times and Ephemera

Edited by
Bryan Brown

Routledge & Kegan Paul
London, Boston and Henley

First published in 1973
by Routledge & Kegan Paul Ltd
39 Store Street
London WC1E 7DD,
Broadway House, Newtown Road
Henley-on-Thames, Oxon RG9 1EN and
9 Park Street
Boston, Mass. 02108, USA
First published as a paperback in 1980
Printed in Great Britain by
W. S. Cowell Ltd, Butter Market, Ipswich
© Bryan Brown 1973

ISBN 0 7100 7542 1 (c)
ISBN 0 7100 0557 1 (p)

Contents

For my Mother

Preface

When I first discovered the work of the Oxford photographer Henry William Taunt, some four years ago, it came as a great surprise to find no published material on either his work or his life. From my reading of contemporary opinion it has become evident that Taunt's work was well respected and popular. The opinion is more than justified for his photographs are outstanding at many levels.

An obituary notice in the *Oxford Chronicle* of 1922 states, 'His lamented death removes a well known figure from Oxford, but his numerous works will form a valuable and standing memorial of his zeal and industry.' It is now fifty years since his death and very little has been done to put Taunt's work into the position of historical importance it so rightly deserves.

Taunt's mastery of photography and his astute sense of scene and composition make him one of the most important but neglected photographers of the last century. Primarily he was a landscape and architectural photographer, but as a keen observer of human nature he took many vivid and characteristic portraits. Perhaps the most important quality of his work is the combination of his talents as artist and social historian, for it provides us with such an enjoyable and informative record of Taunt's age.

To my delight I found a publisher who was of the same opinion as myself and during the last year I have brought together a selection of photographs which conveys a proper sense of Taunt's quality – a quality which I have tried to evoke in the design of the book and the presentation of the photographs in sepia, the colour faithful to Taunt's original conception. I have grouped the photographs into seven main sections, which cover the nature and scope of Taunt's work. First, there is his great love, the Thames; second, Oxford, the place of his birth and death; third, the neighbouring counties to which he frequently travelled; fourth, the places which he visited further afield; fifth, his splendid portraits; sixth, a cross-section of his work in which we can see the images of life of a hundred years ago; and finally, a selection of his humorous and entertaining ephemera. As an introduction to this selection of photographs and to help the reader to put Taunt's life and work into its historical perspective, I have related a little of his character, his history and surroundings and said something about the photographic methods and equipment which Taunt used in the pursuit of his art and craft.

Oxford   Bryan Brown

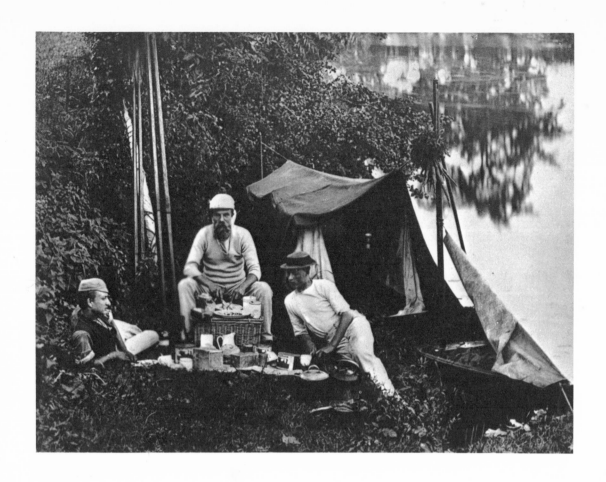

1 'Camping out in a quiet corner'. This shows Taunt's tented boat prepared for one of his river trips, which sometimes lasted three months. The photograph was taken near Barford Mill on the Avon.

Introduction

Henry William Taunt is an almost perfect example of a true Victorian character. His life is full of all the richness, idiosyncrasy and contradiction associated with the reign which covered the greater part of his life. Primarily a photographer, he was also a sound businessman of real enterprise. He never made a fortune, but he developed his establishment, Henry W. Taunt and Company, to a considerable size and ran it successfully for over fifty years. He was a writer and antiquarian of great enthusiasm, writing over fifty books, publishing and printing many of them himself. He was an entertainer, travelling near and far with his magic lantern and slides of his own making. As a musician, he wrote a revised edition of the National Anthem, several political songs and jingles. As a politician he took a keen interest in the affairs of the nation and of the city of Oxford. Official of the Ancient Order of Druids and of the Foresters' Friendly Society, churchman, organist, naturalist, cartographer – there seems little to which he did not turn his hand.

Early Years

Taunt was born on the evening of 14 June 1842 in Pensons Gardens, St Ebbe's, Oxford. Victoria had been on the throne since 1837 and the idea of an Empire was beginning to form. It was the age of the adventurer, the 'Jack of all Trades', the man of energy and enterprise, the character that Taunt so fully embodied. The Great Exhibition of 1851 was to herald the popularization of photography and ten years later, in 1861, the number of commercial photographers had grown from 51 to over 2,500. Such was the competition that Taunt was to face. Oxford business was no less hectic. Life revolved around the University which supported the majority of the working population and many trades and businesses.

Taunt's birth coincided with the introduction of daguerreotypes to England. In 1841 the studios of Richard Beard and Antoine Claudet had been established in London and that of William Constable in Brighton. He was born into a world where a new invention and art form was at the beginning of its most fruitful development, a development in which he was to play his part.

This, however, was a far cry from Pensons Gardens. The Taunts were certainly not wealthy. But they were respected and respectable Victorian citizens. His father was a plumber, glazier and painter with a small business in nearby Bridge Street. Taunt passed most of his young life in the St Ebbe's area, spending his holidays at West Ilsley in the Berkshire Downs, where his mother's parents lived. He recalled the local children, the village school and a schoolmistress whom he liked.

Life was hard for a working-class family in the 1840s, when boys had to begin work young to help support the family. Taunt seems to have received little formal education. He was taught at a church school in St Ebbe's, at West Ilsley and at Evesham in Worcestershire where the family had relations. By the time he was ten he was working for an established Oxford tailor, James Embling of 23 High Street. It was here, in the back of the shop, that Taunt started to read and sometimes paint in watercolours. His wages were four shillings per week. He soon moved on and had further jobs in 'the High' – the hub of Oxford business in the mid-nineteenth century.

His second job was with Henry Ladd, a stationer and newsagent at 10 High Street. Taunt recalled, 'The chief duties were to keep three different sets of customers going with the *Times*, lent to read. Each was supposed to have their paper one hour, but there was no margin of time allowed between to effect the change, and this led into endless difficulties, particularly as some customers wanted to crib more than their time sometimes.'

His next job was with Charles Richards, the High Street bookshop and auctioneers mentioned in Cuthbert Bede's Oxford novel, *The Adventures of Mr Verdant Green* (1853). Here undergraduates sold off the belongings collected during term-time. Taunt relates how Oxford business was dependent on the students and that they were bad at paying their debts:

> There's the story of Joy, the tailor, of Park Street – a man named Heaviness of Wadham owed him an a/c, and was leaving at the end of term. Joy got into the college and caught him. His client received him most graciously, asked him to sit down, told him he was arranging to pay everybody tomorrow, and if Joy would call at 10 in the morning, he would find himself all right. Joy, of course, was delighted as the bill was a heavy one. He went at 10 sharp, went up to the man's room and found him gone. But a note lay on the table addressed: 'Mr Joy with Mr Heaviness' compliments'. He opened it. Inside was a long slip of paper like a cheque, but instead of the magic, 'Pay Mr Joy', it contained these words: 'Heaviness endureth for a night and Joy cometh in the morning'. Too bad.

Enters Photography

At the age of fourteen, in 1856, Taunt made an all-important move and took a job with Edward Bracher, photographic artist of 26 High Street. In the development of Bracher's studio is the early history of photography in Oxford. Bracher, like many of the photographers working in the 1850s, was concerned mostly with portraits and commissioned landscapes. Taunt's reminiscences give us a clear picture of what a typical photographer's studio was like:

> It was a poor little place, with a very narrow staircase lit with a gasjet in one place and very steep up; first to the specimen room into which everybody was asked, then into the dressing

room above that, and lastly up into the gallery. None of the rooms were large enough to swing round the proverbial cat, but Dons and Laity and Ladies and Gentlemen of every class all made their way up these squeaking stairs to be Daguerrotyped at £2.2.0 a time at first, or later to have Positives (pictures on Glass) taken and put into Passepartouts and framed in gaudy ornamental frames.

The daguerreotype that Taunt mentions was the first successful photographic process, introduced in 1839 by the Frenchman Louis Daguerre, whereby the photographic image was made on the surface of a metal plate. The limitation of this method was that only one image was achieved; the client had to be satisfied with his portrait on a unique and beautiful silvered plate. The daguerreotype was superseded by the wet collodion process, made available in 1851 by Frederick Scott Archer, where the picture was taken on a glass plate. This was a great breakthrough as negatives were made and many paper prints could be taken from the original, or the plate could be used as a positive by backing it with dark material thus imitating the daguerreotype. Paper negatives (calotypes) had been produced in the 1840s by Fox Talbot and others, but had many disadvantages. So the advent of the wet collodion process marked the beginning of photography as we know it today. These techniques had created a demand for photographs in the home, and Bracher's studio supplied both *cartes-de-visite* for the family album and stereoscopic cards which were used in the drawing-room viewer. *Cartes-de-visite* were little portraits on a mount the size of a visiting card (Plate 166b), and stereoscopic views were two prints of the same view, taken at a slightly different angle, mounted together on card; viewed through a stereoscope there was a three-dimensional illusion (Plate 63).

Inside the studio the client went through a harassing experience. Sitting in a fixed position, neck in a neck clamp, for the long exposure, one had to suffer the smell of the chemicals and the temperament of the photographer. Nevertheless, Bracher, like many of the early photographers, found business brisk and profitable. While Bracher himself looked after the shop, Taunt began as a utility hand, polishing silvered plates for daguerreotypes or cleaning glass for positives, tasks calling for great care and scrupulous cleanliness. In 1858, at the tender age of sixteen, Taunt was to graduate to the status of photographer. Bracher gave him responsibility for the outdoor work and he began taking stereoscopic views and small groups. It was during this period that Taunt developed his interest in the Thames. Some of his finest photographs of the river were taken in the 1860s, when in his late teens and early twenties. They were taken purely for himself, and show a remarkable awareness of his newly-learned techniques in recording the landscape which he had grown to love.

However, profits from the collodion work were much less than on daguerreotypes and Bracher sold his business. The turnover in photographers at this time was considerable, many taking it up for a quick profit and practising in the simplest of premises. Yet Taunt thrived in such a competitive environment. In 1863, the year of his marriage, Taunt took the job as photographic manager to Wheeler & Day, the stationers to whom Bracher sold his business. Here he learnt more of accountancy and the general know-how of trading, a useful training for his own photographic business, which he started in 1868 at 67 George Street, Oxford. The following year, aged twenty-seven, he moved to new premises at 33 Cornmarket Street, a shop previously occupied by another Oxford photographer.

His work at this time was mostly concerned with *cartes-de-visite* and stereoscopic cards. But he soon developed a series of 'Shilling Views' of Oxford, the Thames and the surrounding countryside. The *Oxford Times* of 23 January 1869 praised his enterprise: 'We have inspected many of these views and have found them most faithful and artistic. All the impressions which we examined were exquisite and evidently most carefully executed.'

Taking a Photograph

It can help us to appreciate the quality of Taunt's work if we understand something about the actual labour of taking a photograph by the wet collodion method. One can imagine Taunt on the river. Precariously positioned in mid-stream, his head shrouded by a black cloth, steadying the heavy camera and bulky tripod, he was ready to capture the scene. The glass plate had to be kept wet the whole time, and outdoors a dark tent was needed for processing the plates on the spot, as we can see in Plate 9 . So Taunt had to carry bottles of chemicals, developing dishes and other paraphernalia to produce his negatives. The quality and detail in his work is not so much due to the lens but to his dexterity in handling the plate and chemicals, and his understanding of the qualities and effects of light, for exposures could vary from five seconds to as long as two minutes. At this time photography could be a hit-or-miss procedure. The long exposure had some strange effects, as in the lovely photograph of Putney Bridge (Plate 52), where we can see the movement of water whilst the bridge and background are sharp. In fact it was possible for someone to walk quickly across a scene being photographed without appearing at all in the photograph itself!

The process was not always complete at the negative stage and many early photographers had various tricks when making their prints. One of Taunt's favourite techniques with a rather bleak-looking scene was to add a dramatic sky. He kept a stock of special sky negatives for this very purpose; an example of this is Plate 17. Another trick was the vignette, a method of making a print with a soft halo around the image area. This enabled Taunt to conceal the fact that the negative was often weak at the edges due to the difficulty in coating the collodion evenly on to the glass plate. We can see this in Plate 125.

Taunt the Entertainer

In 1871 Taunt launched his successful career as an entertainer with a lecture at the Oxford Churchmen's Union on 19 January, on his favourite subject, 'A trip down the Thames from its source to London'. Its success can be judged by the fact that in a revised form it ran at the London Polytechnic for over two hundred nights. The entertainment was carried out with a magic lantern, a splendid mahogany and brass projector which magnified Taunt's glass lantern slides on to a wall at the far end of the room. The lantern show was one of the main sources of public entertainment in the last century. Slides were supplemented by readings which often formed complete stories and were sometimes acted out by performers. The quality of entertainment depended largely on the skill of the lanternist and the humour and personality of the lecturer. In these arts Taunt was a master.

In 1872 Taunt started to lecture professionally and toured the surrounding countryside. He added music to the entertainment, sang the solo or character parts himself and contributed a full repertoire of his own tales and anecdotes. The light which Taunt employed to aid the projection of his slides, oxy-hydrogen limelight, would today no doubt be considered highly dangerous. It consisted of burning a mixture of oxygen and hydrogen on the surface of a cylinder of lime, which became hot and emitted a very white light. However, skilfully handled, it enabled Taunt to show not only slides but chromatropes and other optical novelties, in strong bright colours.

Taunt became a wonderfully accomplished magic-lantern performer, ranging over a variety of subjects. He produced his own slides, beautifully made and coloured in his own workshops, and he wrote many of the readings. His photographic slides of this time are very early examples (Plate 164c). He was famous for his light-hearted entertainments for children. Sometimes there were over a thousand in his audience at the Oxford town hall. Among the amusing titles of the children's tales are 'The Fiddler and the Crocodile', 'Mr O'Toole and his Umbrella', 'The House that Jack built' and 'Hookey beak the Raven – That Raven wasn't good' (Plates 164a–b). More serious addresses were given under the auspices of the Oxford Architectural and Historical Society of which he was a life-long member and for many years official photographer.

During this period Taunt began writing and publishing. His first and best known book, *A New Map of the River Thames from Oxford to London*, came out in 1872. It was during the 1870s that he started to travel more widely, visiting most of the counties of southern England. The *Stratford-upon-Avon Herald* of 24 August 1874 tells of a novelty attraction, Mr Taunt and party camping out in a field near a bridge, with a most peculiar way of preparing the boat for sleeping, as we can see (Plate 1). Taunt's method was probably considered strange, as a more popular way of camping out at that time was with a tent pitched by the riverside. However, Taunt was quite firm in his preference for camping out in his 'Company boat', a twenty-two-foot, broad gig, in which he made most of his early river trips. The newspaper related that he was engaged in taking a series of views of the river Avon and places of interest on the banks which the paper hoped to print. He was also preparing an illustrated entertainment, 'A trip down the Avon'.

Taunt and his Subjects

In considering Taunt's outdoor photography it is important to remember the strong relationship between the photographer and his subject. I have previously mentioned the studio, where the client was literally fixed in position. But outdoors, and especially in the countryside where Taunt frequently worked, the relationship took on a completely different character. In the 1860s and 70s the countryfolk of the Chilterns and Cotswolds had rarely if ever seen a photographer, so the presence of Mr Taunt, his camera and assistants was an unusual spectacle. Taunt's reminiscence of the old lady at King's Weir which I have noted in the caption to Plate 18, must have been typical. Many early photographs are very obviously posed, imitating the Dutch seventeenth-century style of painting (then well known in prints which were sold widely). The bulky equipment, the length of time taken by the photographer to prepare his subject in the composition, his final dive behind a black cloth, the feverish manipulation of the glass plates and slides, must have been a fascinating spectacle. But it sometimes led to rather stilted results as the people stood awkwardly, consciously looking into or away from the camera. However, most of Taunt's photographs have a remarkable freshness and individuality about them. Although not unaware of the photographic equipment, his subjects seem to take up poses natural to their age, character and occupation. Look at the children playing in the brook at Cowley Marsh (Plate 127). Their childish fascination for the camera has enabled Taunt to capture them at their playful frolics; or the boxers at the booth at St Giles Fair (Plate 82), standing with the rigidity of soldiers, showing their muscularity, the requisites of their occupation, to their best advantage.

Similarly it is worth while studying how Taunt composes ordinary scenes and ordinary people in situations to create photographs that are not only valuable social documents, but as visual statements form works of art. A fine example is his photograph of the river at London

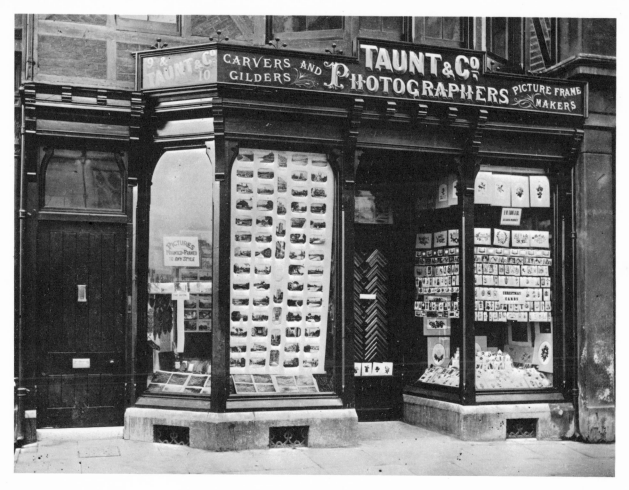

2   The shop in Broad Street, Oxford, which Taunt occupied from 1874 until 1895.

Bridge (Plate 55). His use of the patterned stonework of the bridge forms a strong frame for the steamers and barges, a compositional treatment which might well belong to a much later date.

Taunt's Later Career

After Taunt's successful early beginnings at Bracher's, and the quick establishment of his own business, he progressed quickly and moved to specially prepared premises at 9 and 10 Broad Street, Oxford. He stayed here from 1874 until 1895, and his output of this period includes many of his finest photographs. His was not the meteoric rise of a young Oxford intellectual, lecturing and writing in academic style. It was the rise of a young man self taught, with a deep love of nature, lecturing and writing in the only way he knew, often rather unsophisticatedly and sentimentally, for which he was sometimes criticized and ribbed when lecturing to University audiences. Nevertheless, he provided real insight and entertainment to all who came to his lectures or read his books.

As an astute businessman he diversified his activities. He opened a glass salesroom, a picture-framing, carving and gilding establishment and a bicycle shop. A well-known cyclist himself, renowned for his three-wheeled machines, he advertised his shop thus: 'Gentlemen passing through Oxford can leave their machines and have them put straight.' He further extended his photographic business by opening another shop in High Wycombe.

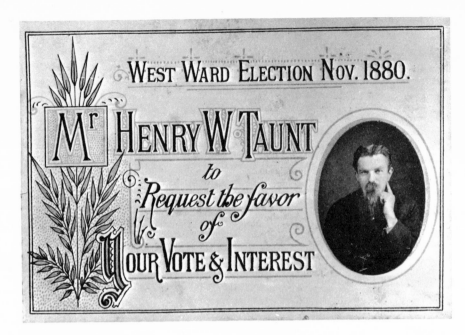

3 Henry Taunt's election card, used to promote himself standing as an Independent candidate in the Oxford local election of 1880.

Locally Taunt was well known as an active politician, 'a doughty and chivalrous fighter', as the *Oxford Chronicle* remembered him in its obituary notice. In 1880 Taunt stood as an Independent candidate in the local election on the issues of a clean water supply and the formation of a local Ratepayers' Association. Characteristically he distributed his promotional material far and wide. Unfortunately, he was unsuccessful, and again the following year. But he continued to take a lively interest in local politics and at regular intervals produced posters and leaflets concerning 'Things to be put right' for the general good of the community. Later, between 1908 and 1922, the year of his death, he issued a bulletin which carried his thoughts on local affairs. He called it *Notes and News from Oxford's Famous City*. Through this Taunt continued his political activity, battling with local councillors about the way in which they ran the affairs of the city and leading campaigns, some of which were highly successful, against the introduction of electric trams, the excessive charges of the Great Western Railway, the rise in local rates and the dumping of 'snow and muck' near his home.

Taunt was of striking appearance. A tall, bearded figure, locally known as 'Skelly', he was not unlike George Bernard Shaw. He was a familiar sight in Oxford and is especially remembered for his appearance during Eights Week, selling photographs of the crew and race charts at his stall. This great Oxford character was also a leading light in most of the social functions of the city. He was organist and leader of the choir at his local church of St Mary Magdalen in Magdalen Street. He was a staunch supporter of the philanthropic societies; an Arch Druid of the Albion Lodge 59 and a leading member of the Foresters. He was also well known for his various modes of transport. On land he travelled on a tricycle, his favourite model a two-seater. Randolph Adams, his assistant for over forty years, sat on the front pedalling the machine, whilst Henry Taunt sat majestically behind with the equipment strapped between the axles. On the river, at first he had the outrigged broad gig. But in time he moved on to a flat-bottomed boat (Frontispiece) which was moored on the Thames opposite the University Boat House. Taunt considered living here a thoroughly 'lotus-eating existence'.

Most of Taunt's activities are marked by his unfailing zest for self-promotion. For this he suffered considerable criticism from his contemporaries. His attitude towards advertising is declared in a verse he quoted on the success of the Beecham advertising campaign in 1914.

> The man who has a thing to sell
> And goes and whispers down a well
> Is not so apt to cop the dollers
> As he who climbs a tree and hollers.

Taunt's Enterprises

Despite his energetic advertising, Taunt suffered a financial setback in 1895, and was taken to the debtors' court. There were a number of reasons, but this was mainly due to the bad debts of the students and an unsatisfactory arrangement with the landlord. Also, 'Do it Yourself' photography was beginning to have an effect. Although prints were still popular and the family album was an essential item of the drawing room until well past the Edwardian era, photography was no longer the preserve of the professionals. It was fast becoming a fashionable pastime for the amateurs. Technical progress had brought the box-camera and roll film. The Eastman catch-phrase of the 1890s summed up the situation, 'Squeeze the ball and we'll do the rest'. However, Taunt was scathing about the results: 'the wretched things are often not pictures, and so photographs have deteriorated to such an extent that they no longer sell, and the ordinary daily papers are stuffed with the productions of the camera – such as they are'.

But he was soon back in business and started trading again in makeshift premises at 41 High Street. Here he stayed for a year, moving to 34 High Street, where he carried on his trade for ten years. However the nature of his business was to change. The half-tone reproduction process, invented in 1883, came into general use about the turn of the century, when the Rotary Photographic Company introduced the photographic picture-postcard to this country. Technical progress necessitates change and Taunt, like many other professional photographers, turned to related enterprises for a living.

It was during the 1890s and early years of this century that Taunt developed 'Rivera', the house and four-acre site on which he had taken a lease in 1889. 'Rivera', named after his associations with the river Thames, is situated at Cowley Marsh, part of the present suburb and past village of Cowley to the east of Oxford. Taunt extended the premises to house not only his extensive photographic unit but also a workshop for type and machines and a handicraft room, which were to provide the manufacturing facilities for the expansion of his publishing activities.

During the last twenty years of his life, Taunt capitalized on the photographic work and experience of forty years, writing and researching with great ability; he produced a vast amount of printed work. Of his fifty books, forty were published during this period. In one year alone he wrote, printed and published no fewer than seven of that total. He always enjoyed the company of academics, and was rewarded for his own scholarship in 1893 by being elected a Fellow of the Royal Geographical Society. He continued to use the letters FRGS after his name until he died, although he resigned from the Society in 1906. He also developed the production of postcards and expanded his lantern slide manufacturing. The postcards were produced in a variety of series including Oxford, the Thames Valley and English Country Life. Among his many publications, his music is notable. Although he called his music and poetry, jingles, they are far more worthy than that title suggests. They include his National Anthem, a Conservative Marching Song, Recruitment Songs for the Great War and collections of folk music.

Taunt's Achievements

Perhaps Taunt was not in the highest sense a genius but his supreme technical ability with the camera was linked to a genuine artistic talent. As well as being creative, he was a man of determination, a strongly individual character. In 1922, the year of his death in his eightieth year, he was to be seen pedalling his tricycle through the streets of Oxford, with all the vigour of his youth. So his enormous achievement of sixty thousand negatives comes as no surprise to us, nor is it a surprise to find that so many of them are masterpieces of photography.

When we turn to evaluate Taunt's work aesthetically, it is his early landscapes which capture the imagination. During his lifetime his photographs were never presented at institutes of art; he was never a member of artistic society. But his work has a charm and beauty in many ways superior to that of his contemporaries. His early work, mostly represented in this selection by photographs taken on the Thames in the 1860s and 70s, is a precious record of nineteenth-century England. The compositions portray the naturalness of the scene, and with the superb detail achieved by Taunt's skill with the wet collodion process, they give a magical illusion of life a hundred years ago. Though until now seldom remembered or appreciated, his extraordinary work, covering a period of over sixty years, shows his very real abilities. Unfortunately much of Taunt's work, as with many of the early photographers who worked with glass, was destroyed after his death, but enough exists for us to form an opinion. His photographs form a heritage which I hope all will enjoy who see them reproduced here.

The Thames

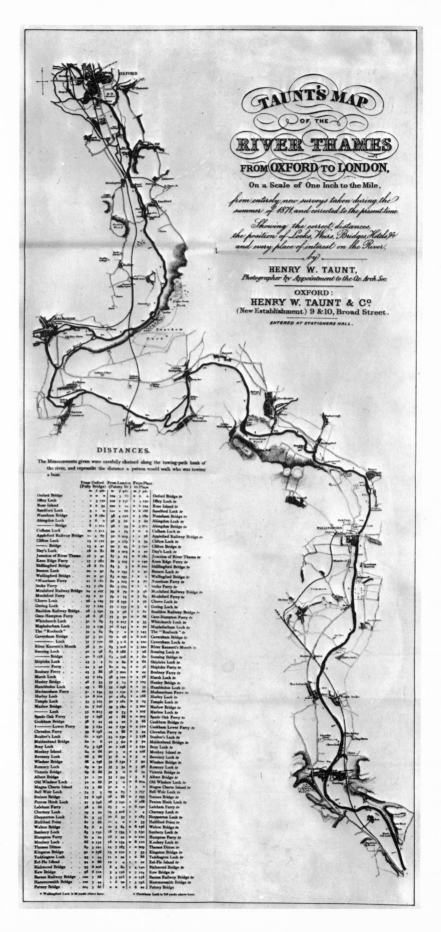

4, 5, 6 Taunt's earliest map of the Thames, from Oxford to London, for the use of river travellers, in three sheets.

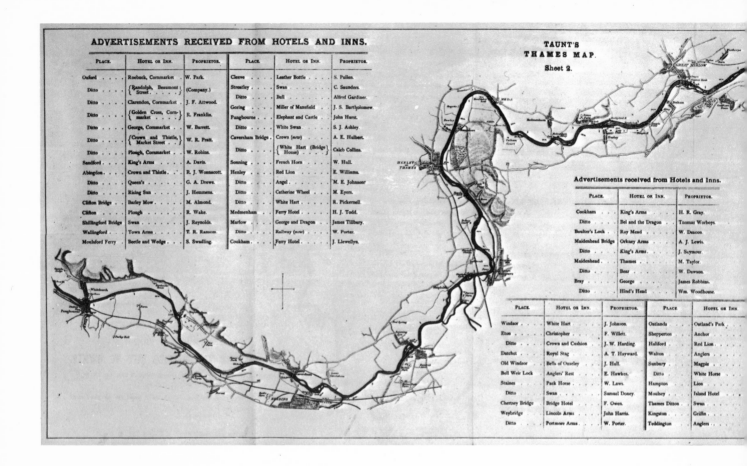

ADVERTISEMENTS RECEIVED FROM HOTELS AND INNS.

PLACE.	HOTEL OR INN.	PROPRIETOR.	PLACE.	HOTEL OR INN.	PROPRIETOR.
Oxford	Roebuck, Cornmarket	W. Park.	Cleeve	Leather Bottle	S. Pullen.
Ditto	Randolph, Beaumont Street	(Company.)	Streatley	Swan	C. Saunders.
Ditto	Clarendon, Cornmarket	J. F. Attwood.	Ditto	Bull	Alfred Gardiner.
Ditto	Golden Cross, Cornmarket	R. Franklin.	Goring	Miller of Mansfield	J. S. Bartholomew.
Ditto	George, Cornmarket	W. Barrett.	Pangbourne	Elephant and Castle	John Hurst.
Ditto	Crown and Thistle, Market Street	W. R. Pratt.	Ditto	White Swan	S. J. Ashley.
Ditto	Plough, Cornmarket	W. Robins.	Caversham Bridge	Crown (new)	A. E. Hulbert.
Sandford	King's Arms	A. Davis.	Ditto	White Hart (Bridge House)	Caleb Collins.
Abingdon	Crown and Thistle	R. J. Wonnacott.	Sonning	French Horn	W. Hull.
Ditto	Queen's	G. A. Drewe.	Henley	Red Lion	E. Williams.
Ditto	Rising Sun	J. Hemmens.	Ditto	Angel	M. E. Johnson.
Clifton Bridge	Barley Mow	M. Almond.	Ditto	Catherine Wheel	M. Eyers.
Clifton	Plough	R. Wake.	Ditto	White Hart	R. Pickernell.
Shillingford Bridge	Swan	J. Reynolds.	Medmenham	Ferry Hotel	H. J. Todd.
Wallingford	Town Arms	T. R. Ransom.	Marlow	George and Dragon	James Tillbury.
Moulsford Ferry	Beetle and Wedge	S. Swadling.	Ditto	Railway (new)	W. Porter.
			Cookham	Ferry Hotel	J. Llewellyn.

TAUNT'S THAMES MAP. Sheet 2.

Advertisements received from Hotels and Inns.

PLACE.	HOTEL OR INN.	PROPRIETOR.
Cookham	King's Arms	H. R. Gray.
Ditto	Bel and the Dragon	Thomas Worboys.
Boulter's Lock	Ray Mead	W. Deacon.
Maidenhead Bridge	Orkney Arms	A. J. Lewis.
Ditto	King's Arms	J. Seymour.
Maidenhead	Thames	M. Taylor.
Ditto	Bear	W. Dawson.
Bray	George	James Robbins.
Ditto	Hind's Head	Wm. Woodhouse.

PLACE.	HOTEL OR INN.	PROPRIETOR.	PLACE.	HOTEL OR INN.
Windsor	White Hart	J. Johnson.	Oatlands	Oatland's Park
Eton	Christopher	F. Willett.	Shepperton	Anchor
Ditto	Crown and Cushion	J. W. Harding.	Halliford	Red Lion
Datchet	Royal Stag	A. T. Hayward.	Walton	Anglers
Old Windsor	Bells of Ouseley	J. Hull.	Sunbury	Magpie
Bell Weir Lock	Anglers' Rest	E. Hawkes.	Ditto	White Horse
Staines	Pack Horse	W. Laws.	Hampton	Lion
Ditto	Swan	Samuel Doney.	Moulsey	Island Hotel
Chertsey Bridge	Bridge Hotel	F. Owen.	Thames Ditton	Swan
Weybridge	Lincoln Arms	John Harris.	Kingston	Griffin
Ditto	Portmore Arms	W. Porter.	Teddington	Anglers

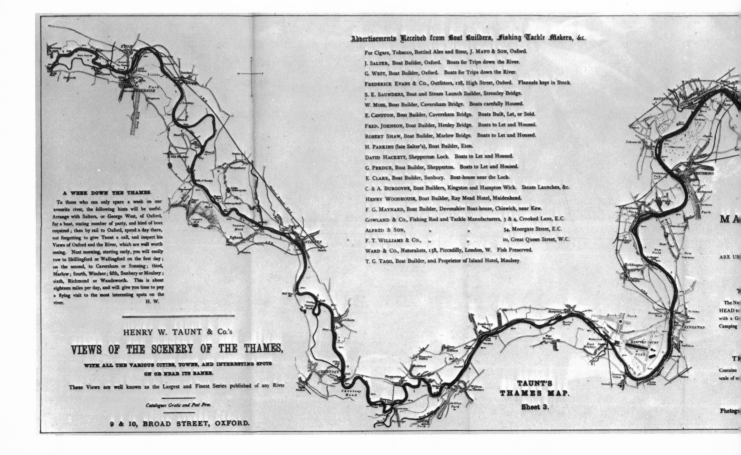

Advertisements Received from Boat Builders, Fishing Tackle Makers, &c.

For Cigars, Tobacco, Bottled Ales and Stout, J. MAYO & SON, Oxford.

J. SALTER, Boat Builder, Oxford. Boats for Trips down the River.

G. WEST, Boat Builder, Oxford. Boats for Trips down the River.

FREDERICK EVANS & CO., Outfitters, 128, High Street, Oxford. Flannels kept in Stock.

S. E. SAUNDERS, Boat and Steam Launch Builder, Streatley Bridge.

W. MOSS, Boat Builder, Caversham Bridge. Boats carefully Housed.

E. CAWSTON, Boat Builder, Caversham Bridge. Boats Built, Let, or Sold.

FRED. JOHNSON, Boat Builder, Henley Bridge. Boats to Let and Housed.

ROBERT SHAW, Boat Builder, Marlow Bridge. Boats to Let and Housed.

H. PARKINS (late Salter's), Boat Builder, Eton.

DAVID HACKETT, Shepperton Lock. Boats to Let and Housed.

G. PERDUE, Boat Builder, Shepperton. Boats to Let and Housed.

E. CLARK, Boat Builder, Sunbury. Boat-house near the Lock.

C. & A. BURGOYNE, Boat Builders, Kingston and Hampton Wick. Steam Launches, &c.

HENRY WOODHOUSE, Boat Builder, Ray Mead Hotel, Maidenhead.

F. G. MAYNARD, Boat Builder, Devonshire Boat-house, Chiswick, near Kew.

GOWLAND & CO., Fishing Rod and Tackle Manufacturers, 3 & 4, Crooked Lane, E.C.

ALFRED & SON, „ „ 54, Moorgate Street, E.C.

F. T. WILLIAMS & CO., „ „ 10, Great Queen Street, W.C.

WARD & CO., Naturalists, 158, Piccadilly, London, W. Fish Preserved.

T. G. TAGG, Boat Builder, and Proprietor of Island Hotel, Moulsey.

A WEEK DOWN THE THAMES.

To those who can only spare a week on our favourite river, the following hints will be useful. Arrange with Salters, or George West, of Oxford, for a boat, stating number of party, and kind of boat required; then by rail to Oxford, spend a day there, not forgetting to give Taunt a call, and inspect his Views of Oxford and the River, which are well worth seeing. Next morning, starting early, you will easily row to Shillingford or Wallingford on the first day; on the second, to Caversham or Sonning; third, Marlow; fourth, Windsor; fifth, Sunbury or Moulsey; sixth, Richmond or Wandsworth. This is about eighteen miles per day, and will give you time to pay a flying visit to the most interesting spots on the river. H.W.

HENRY W. TAUNT & Co.'s
VIEWS OF THE SCENERY OF THE THAMES,
WITH ALL THE VARIOUS CITIES, TOWNS, AND INTERESTING SPOTS ON OR NEAR ITS BANKS.

These Views are well known as the Largest and Finest Series published of any River.

Catalogues Gratis and Post Free.

9 & 10, BROAD STREET, OXFORD.

TAUNT'S THAMES MAP. Sheet 3.

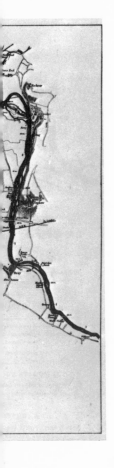

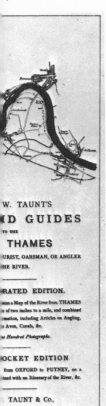

Taunt's lifelong and intimate relationship with the Thames began in 1859, when, inspired by the recently published *Book of the Thames* by Mr and Mrs S. C. Hall, he undertook a journey from Oxford to Cricklade during his Christmas holidays. The journey, in an outrigged dinghy, was a hazardous adventure for a lad of seventeen. The river was in full flood, and the upper reaches with many old locks and weirs proved difficult and sometimes dangerous to navigate.

This early experience was to have great meaning for Taunt, and profoundly affect his photographs of this area taken in future years. The journey introduced him to the river folk and their picturesque riverside dwellings, to the numerous locks, weirs, bridges and inns; for sixty years he was their frequent visitor, recorder and historian.

Of all Taunt's work I find his early photographs of the Thames perhaps the finest. During the years 1860 to 1865 he undertook several trips on the river, and the work of that period has a grace and charm reminiscent of the seventeenth-century school of Dutch landscape painting. He delights in the water-worn timbers of the locks and mills, the combination of flowing water and dark shadowy trees, and the strongly characteristic faces of the river folk.

Like many early photographs, his work of this period relates closely to painting. One can see this in the photographs of Inglesham Round House (Plate 10) or King's Weir (Plate 18); the reflections in the water, the old woman at her humble cottage, each element placed so unerringly in relation to another that nothing could be altered, there is an endless pleasure for the eye in this perfect balance. Varying the length of his exposure, Taunt captures light and water in a sparkling and radiant way. His pictures of Iffley Mill (Plate 21) and Old Putney Bridge (Plate 52) glow with a wealth of light and space.

Another side of Taunt's work is that of the recorder, using the photograph as a social document. During the 1870s the river was discovered by the holiday-maker, and the Thames became a popular resort for Sunday picnics, annual holidays and society functions such as Henley Regatta. His Thames photographs, numbering about fifteen thousand, are the most complete nineteenth-century study of any river. Beginning in 1859, they provide us with a complete visual record of the old river, the river as portrayed by the artists Samuel Ireland and Boydell. His later work illustrates how the river changed from a vital commercial link to a leisure playground; how the locks and weirs were rebuilt and how the riverside customs and way of life altered.

Over the years of his close association with the river, Taunt became an acknowledged and valued historian. Fred S. Thacker, the recognized authority on the Thames, uses many of Taunt's references and first-hand experiences in all three of his standard volumes on the river. In his general history, *The Thames Highway* (1914) when discussing John Taylor, the water poet, he parallels Taunt with Cobbett, the nineteenth-century traveller, famous for his *Rural Rides*. Similarly, Henry Wellington Wack used Taunt photographs as illustrations in his book on the river, *In Thamesland* (1906), and relates that 'Mr Taunt is the dean of Thames Valley students and an ardent lover of river sport.'

Taunt – always alert to a business opportunity – combined his abilities as photographer and historian to write and publish his map and guide to the Thames entitled *A New Map of the River Thames*. This was in fact the earliest photographically illustrated guidebook. The first edition in 1872 came just on the wave of the Thames boom and was rapidly sold out. This book, published in several editions, was written from regular surveys by the author, and gave 'every information required by the Tourist, the Oarsman and the Angler'. The maps drawn and measured by Taunt himself, are beautifully designed, and were drawn to distances carefully chained along the towing-path from Oxford to London. Plates 4, 5, 6 are the maps sold in sheet form.

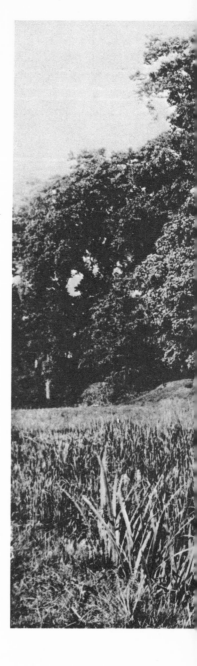

7   Somerford Upper Mill, the first mill on the Thames, near the village of Somerford Keynes in Gloucestershire, *c.* 1885.

8   Hatchet's plank bridge near Cricklade, *c.* 1875, showing a man using a wooden yoke, carrying perhaps two pails of good Thames water for his lady. Cricklade is generally the highest point reached by small boats.

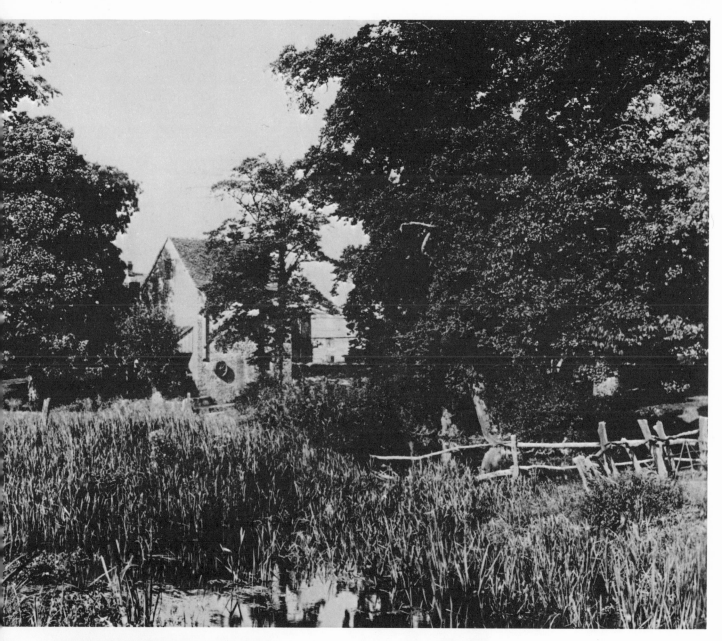

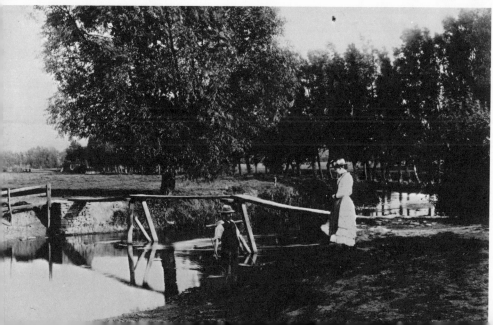

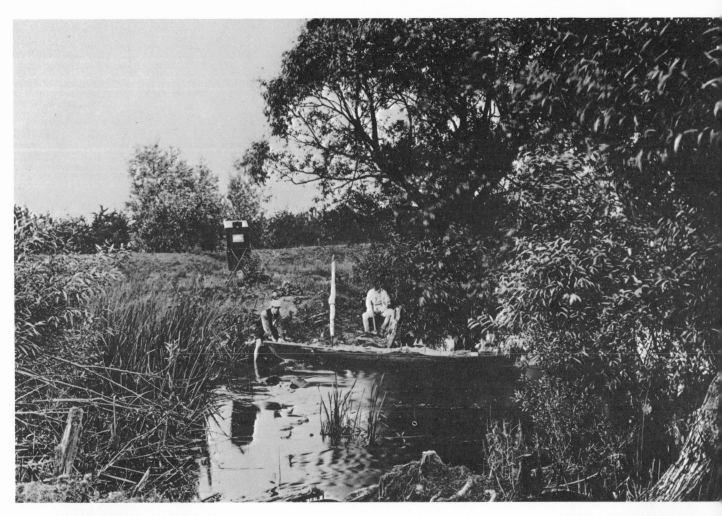

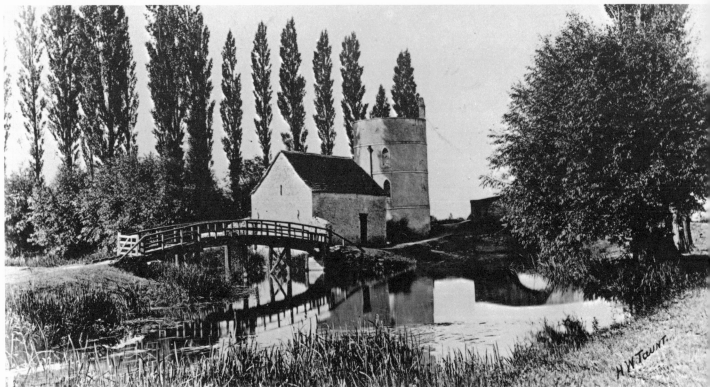

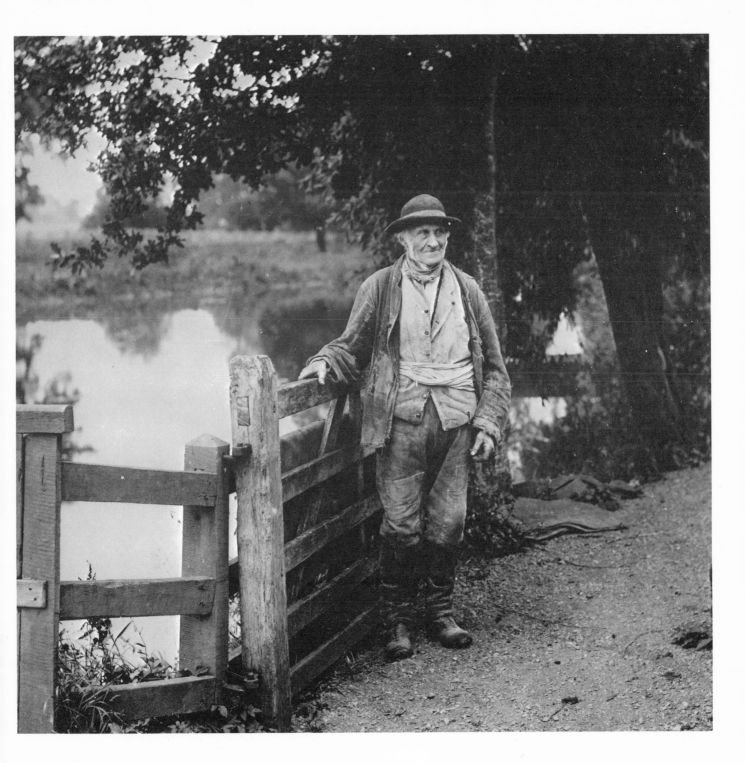

9   A stepping-stone crossing at a small pool below old
Ham Weir in 1863. Young Taunt is at the bow of the
boat with the weir-keeper and his gun. In the background
is the photographic tent for processing the wet collodion
plates.

10   Inglesham Round House at the junction of the
Thames, the Thames & Severn canal, and the Colne,
c. 1863. The round house, the lock-keeper's dwelling, is a
particular feature of this canal. It forms a pleasant view
with the poplars, a group reminiscent of Iffley.

11   A typical old weir-keeper and fisherman, clad in his
corduroy and slop (wide knickerbockers), in 1900. Taunt
mentions, 'What old Harper didn't know about the
weeds, the fish and the wild ducks wasn't worth
knowing, enough to teach the best-read Oxford
professor.'

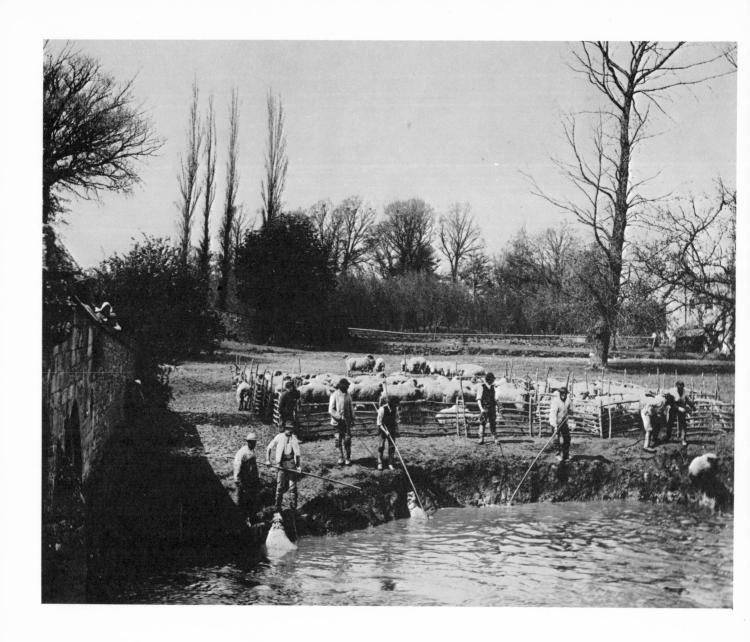

12   Sheep-washing at Radcot Bridge, *c.* 1890. Sheep-rearing was one of the most common methods of farming in this area. The wool was probably sent to Witney, to be made into the famous blankets of that name.

13   Tadpole Bridge, built in 1802, showing a young lady angler and her pet dog, *c.* 1903. Tadpole Bridge, now seemingly in the middle of nowhere, was an important wharf in the early nineteenth century.

14   Duxford Farm and landing place, with a cluster of thatched outhouses and farm buildings, near the old river crossing, *c.* 1860.

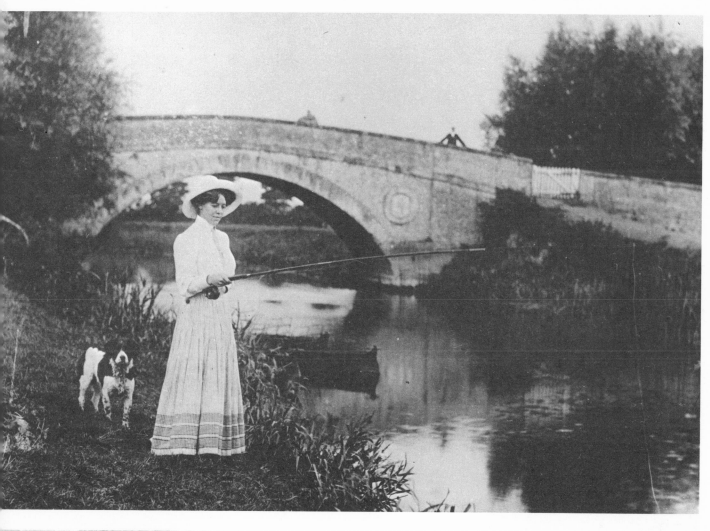
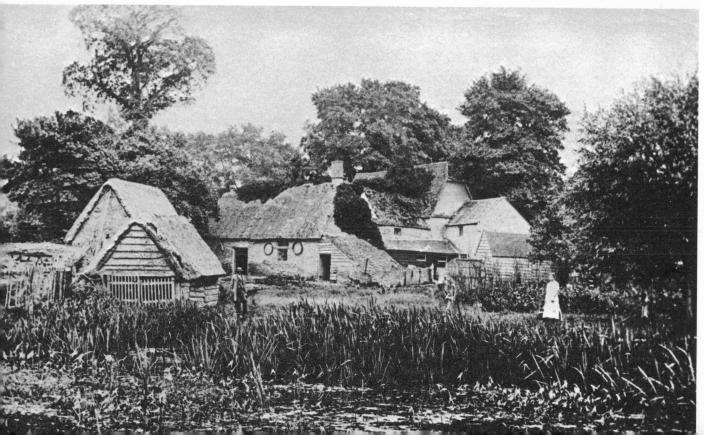

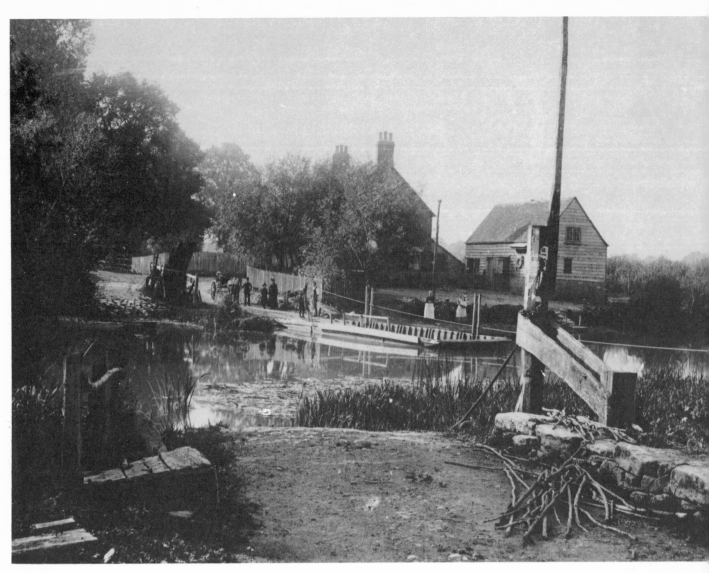

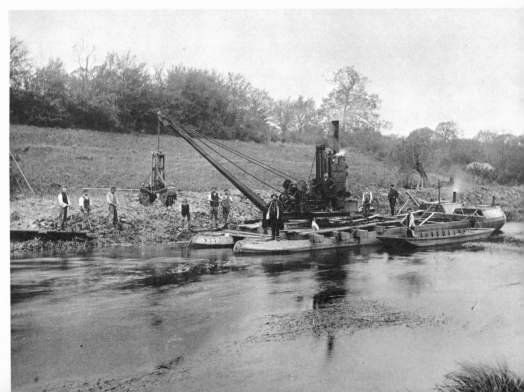

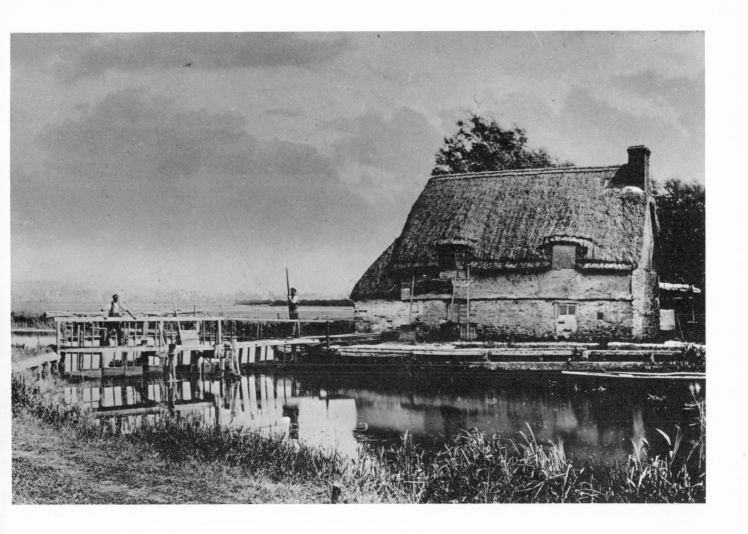

15   Babylockythe ferry, *c.* 1890. The ferry, which linked
Cumnor to Stanton Harcourt, was the last remaining
chain-operated ferry on the Thames, and ceased
working only a few years ago.

16   A Thames Conservancy steam dredger, *c.* 1900,
mounted on timber bulks laid across two narrow boats.
The weight of the dredger is counter-balanced by the
coal in the aft hold of the boats.

17   Skinners' Weir and cottage in 1865. It was a little inn
which had been in the possession of the Skinners from
father to son for many years and the last landlord, Joe
Skinner, on the left of the photograph, was according to
Taunt, 'one of the best-hearted and quaintest fellows
that ever lived'. He is remembered as a typical man of the
barges, and as a tremendous shot with his duck gun. In
winter-time when the floods were out, it is said he took
a bag of nearly forty with one discharge. Today all that
is left is a pool bearing the family name.

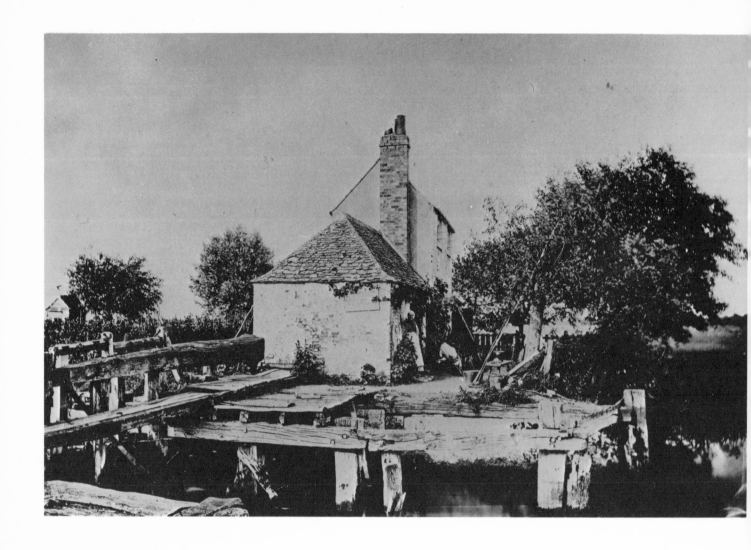

18   King's Weir in 1863 with its double paddle-gates.
The balancing beams, simply two tree trunks, are
somewhat shaved off where they were bolted to the
rymers which held the sluices, but with their heavy butts
left to open the lock. 'The old grandma', Taunt says,
'was wondering what them young fellas are doing, as
cameras in those days were a novelty.' This old 'flash'
lock was not replaced till 1928 when the present King's
Lock was built.

19   Godstow, the Trout Inn, *c.* 1875. Originally the
guest house of St Frideswide's Nunnery, associated with
Fair Rosamund and her lover Henry II.

20   The Medley boat-stations of Bossom and Beesley,
c. 1890, showing the sailing boats which were sailed on
the Port Meadow Reach beyond.

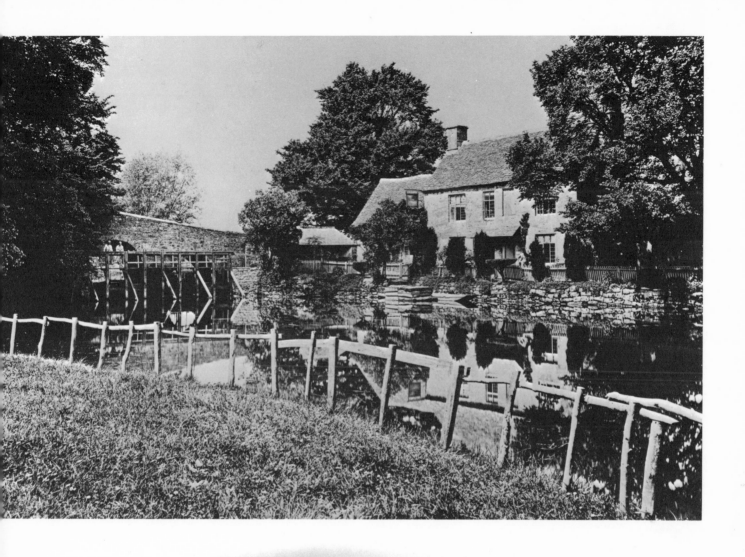

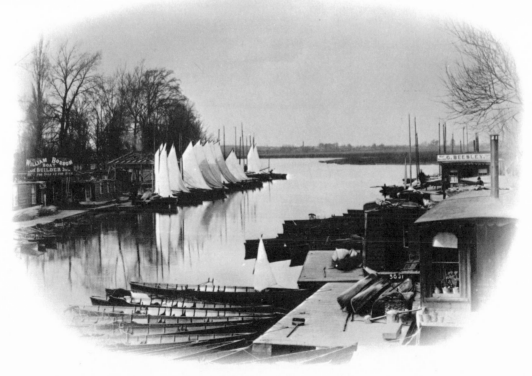

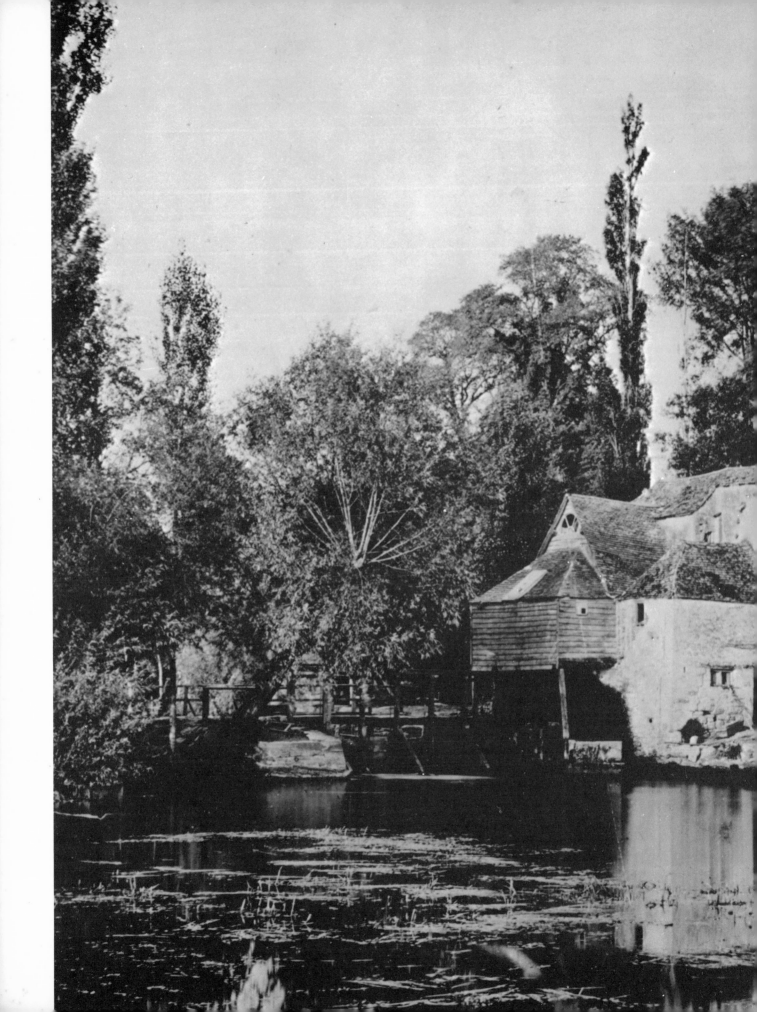

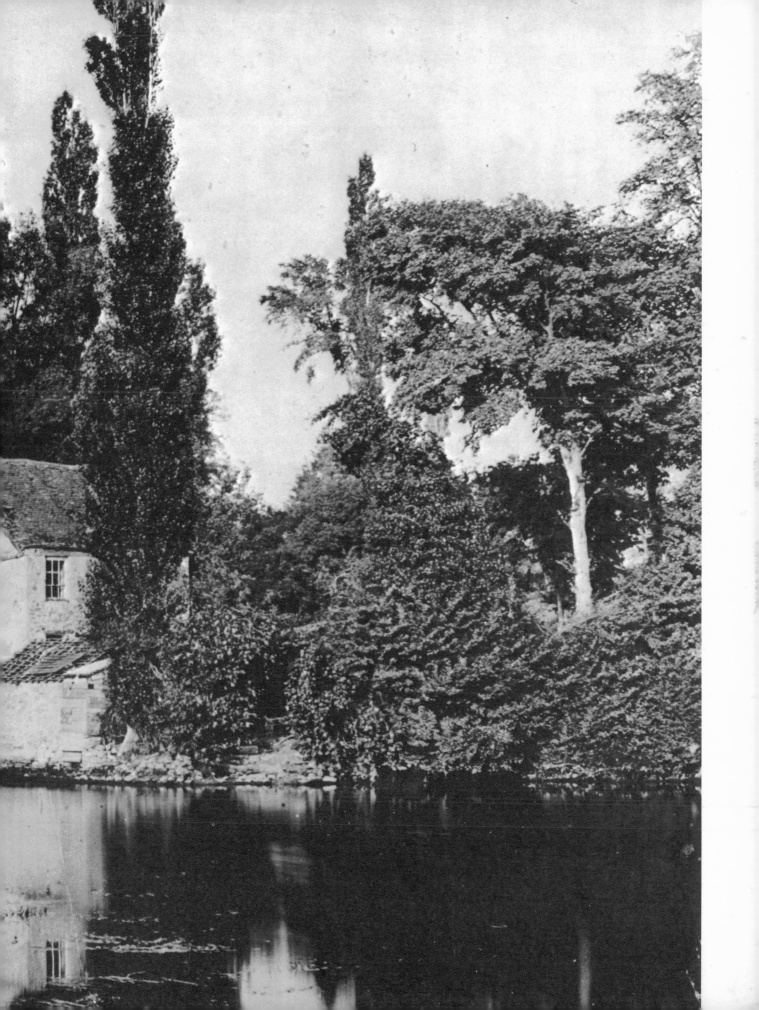

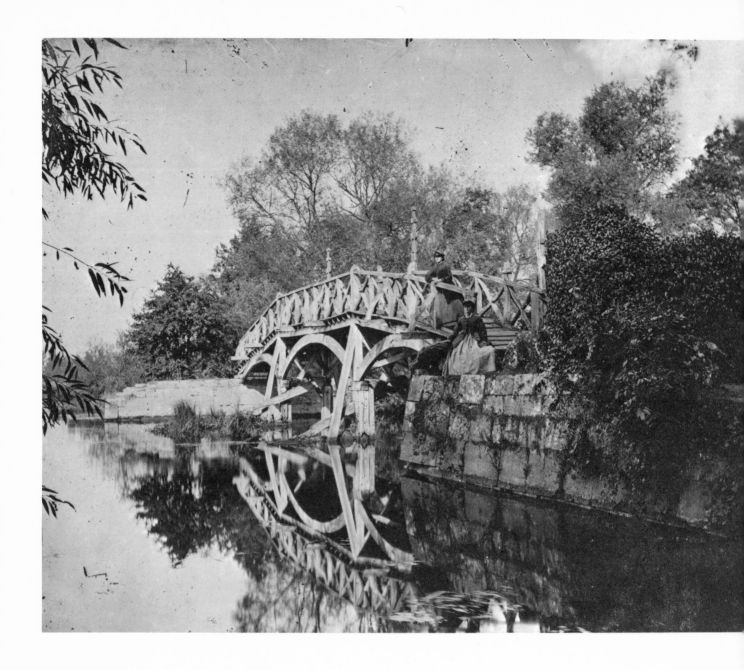

21 *previous page* Iffley mill taken from the river in 1862.
This mill was a place much beloved by artists, for its
enchanting look of splendid neglect. Sadly it was burnt
down in May 1908, and never rebuilt.

22 Nuneham Bridge with two ladies, *c.* 1870. A favourite
place for river jaunts in the 70s; picnic parties were
allowed to land on Tuesdays and Thursdays during the
season. Nuneham was the seat of the Harcourt family. It
now belongs to Oxford University.

23 St Helen's church, Abingdon, from St Helen's
wharf, *c.* 1890. The long disused Berks & Wilts canal
joins the Thames here; Abingdon was an important
centre in the days of water-borne trade.

24 Two boating parties at Day's Lock, showing
Wittenham Clumps in the background, June 1904.

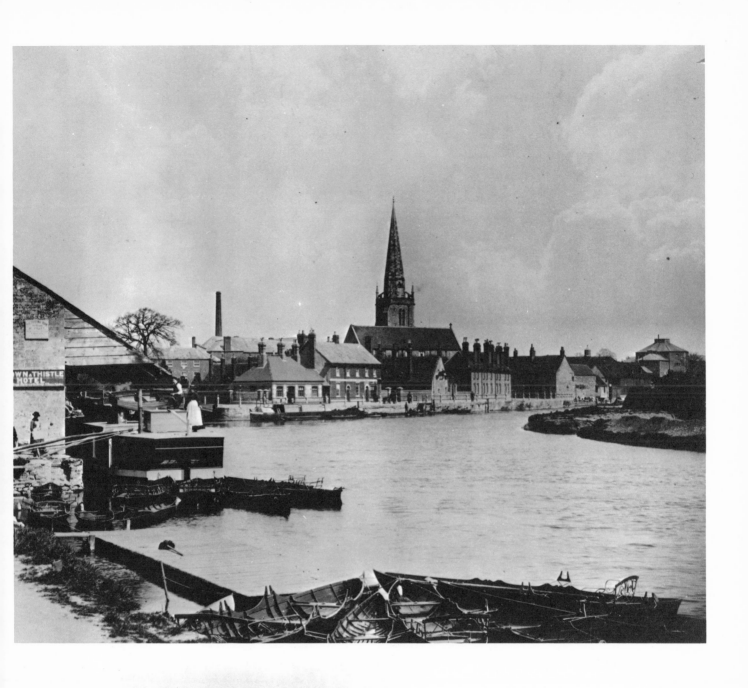

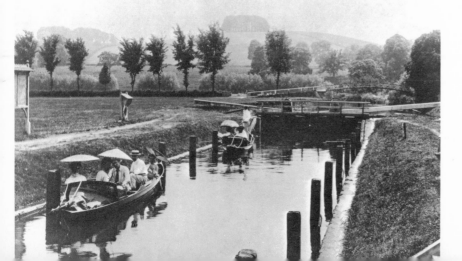

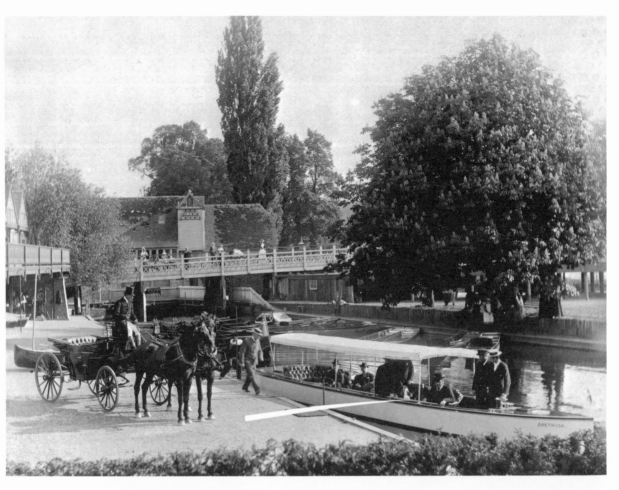

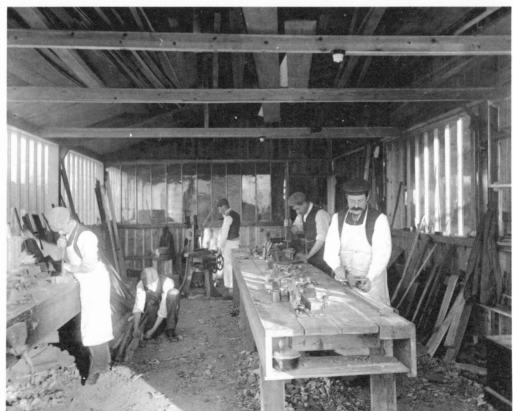

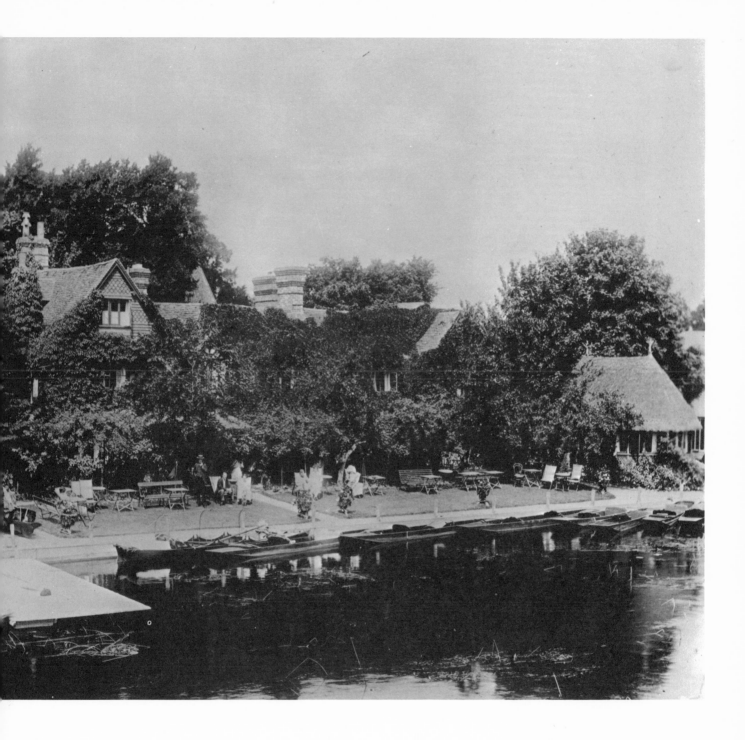

25 S. E. Saunders, the owner of the boat-building business, embarking on a river trip in the late 1890s.

26 The workshops of S. E. Saunders, the Goring boat-builder, in the late 1890s.

27 An ever-popular Thames-side hostelry, the Swan at Streatley, *c.* 1880. An extract from *Punch*, 'Lays of a Lazy Minstrel, A Streatley Sonata':

> I sit and lounge here on the grass,
> And watch the river traffic pass;
> I note a dimpled, fair young lass,
>   Who feathers low and neatly:
> Her hands are brown, her eyes are grey,
> And trim her nautical array –
> Alas! she swiftly sculls away,
>   And leaves the 'Swan' at Streatley!

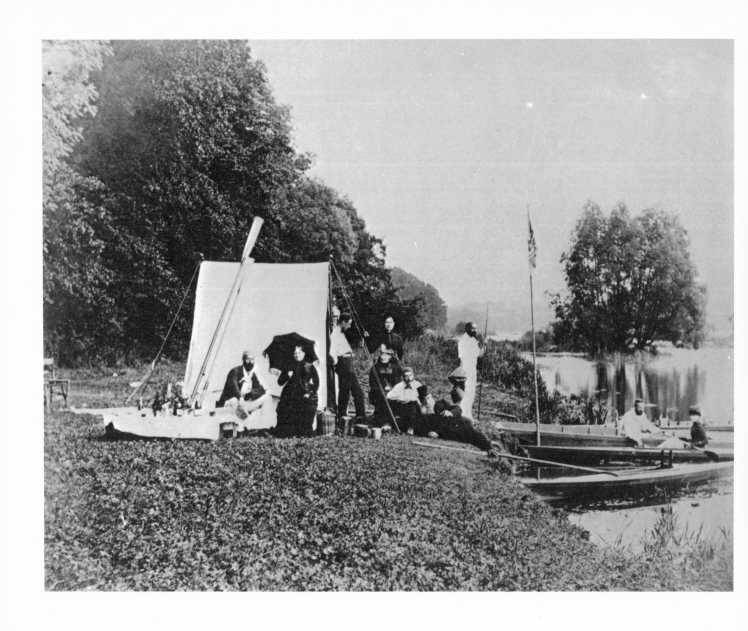

28   A rather special camping party taken at Hart's Wood, *c.* 1880. Note that this is no humble picnic but one with champagne and hampers.

29   A pair of canal or narrow boats passing Shooter's Hill, Pangbourne, *c.* 1890. Such boats, built for use on the narrow canals, were used commercially on the river as well as the wider Thames barges until well into the present century.

30   Eel bucks being emptied at Caversham, taken from the bridge, *c.* 1880. The wicker baskets or pots are raised and lowered on a simple timber framework.

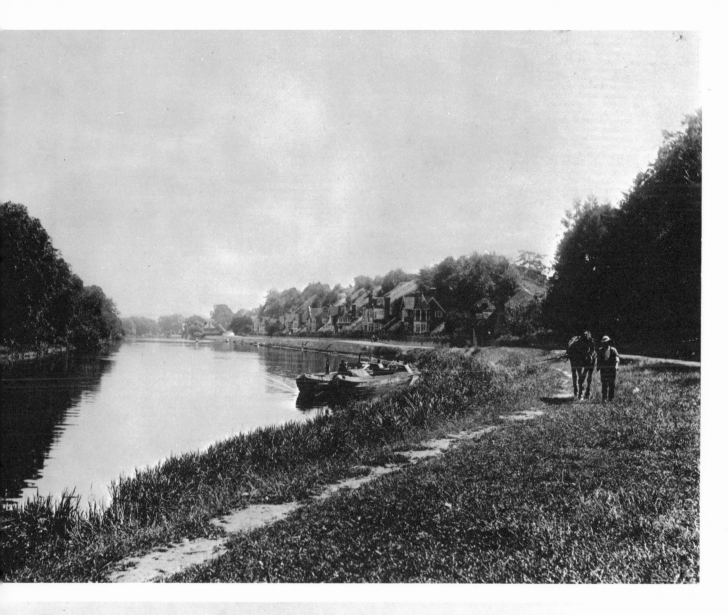

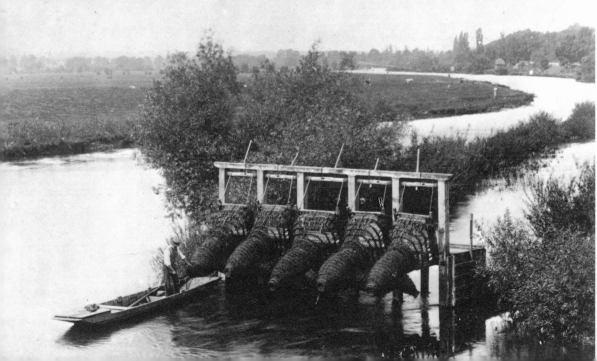

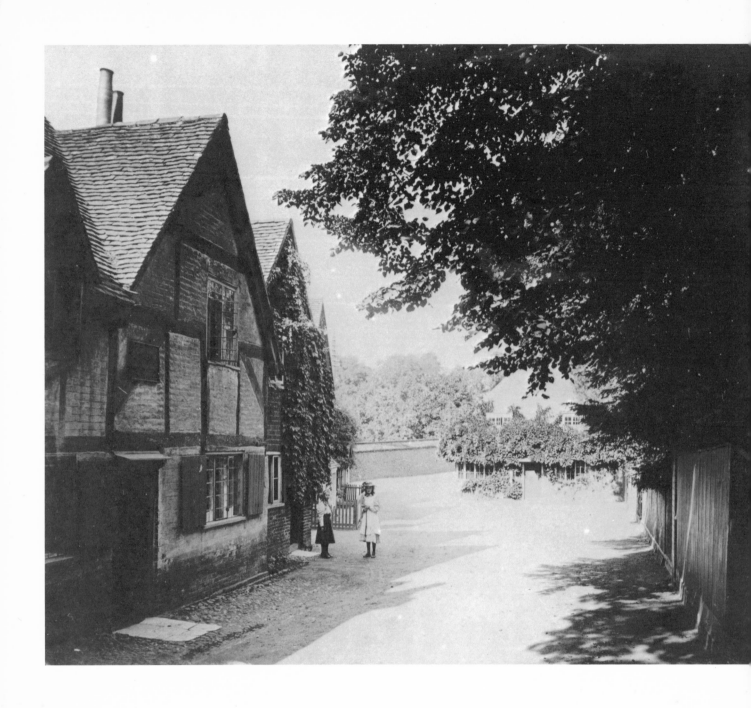

31 A typical Thames village: two girls at the bottom of
Middle Street, Sonning, in the late 1890s.

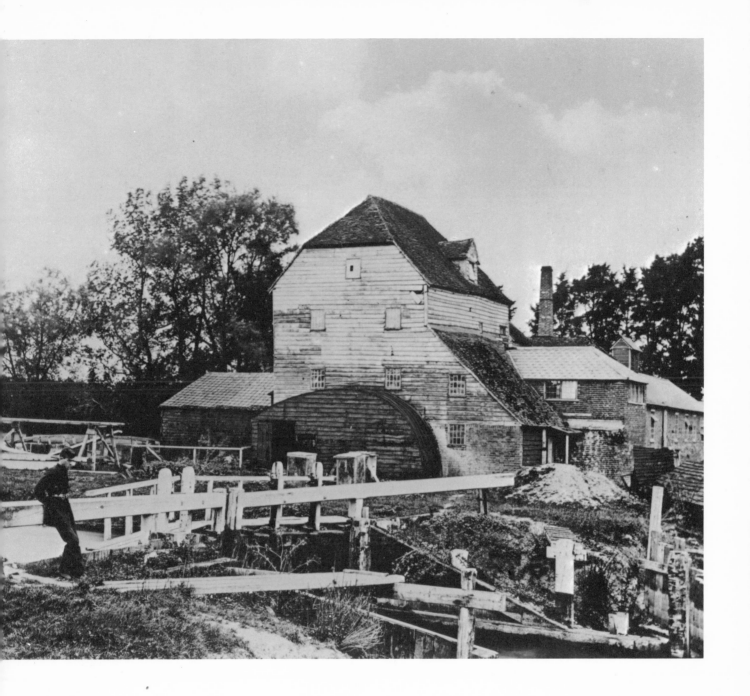

32 Shiplake lock and mill, *c.* 1870. The lock was one of
the first pound locks designed by Humphrey
Gainsborough, brother of the painter, about 1770. These
are the locks in use on the Thames now; a chamber with
two pairs of gates allows the boats to change level. When
the photograph was taken the mill had recently been
boarded up, amidst indignant protests from artists.

33 *following page*   The crush of boats at Henley Regatta
in about 1900. This mass of boats spread itself over
the whole of the course, filling it with a crowd so dense
that it was possible to walk from boat to boat across the
river.

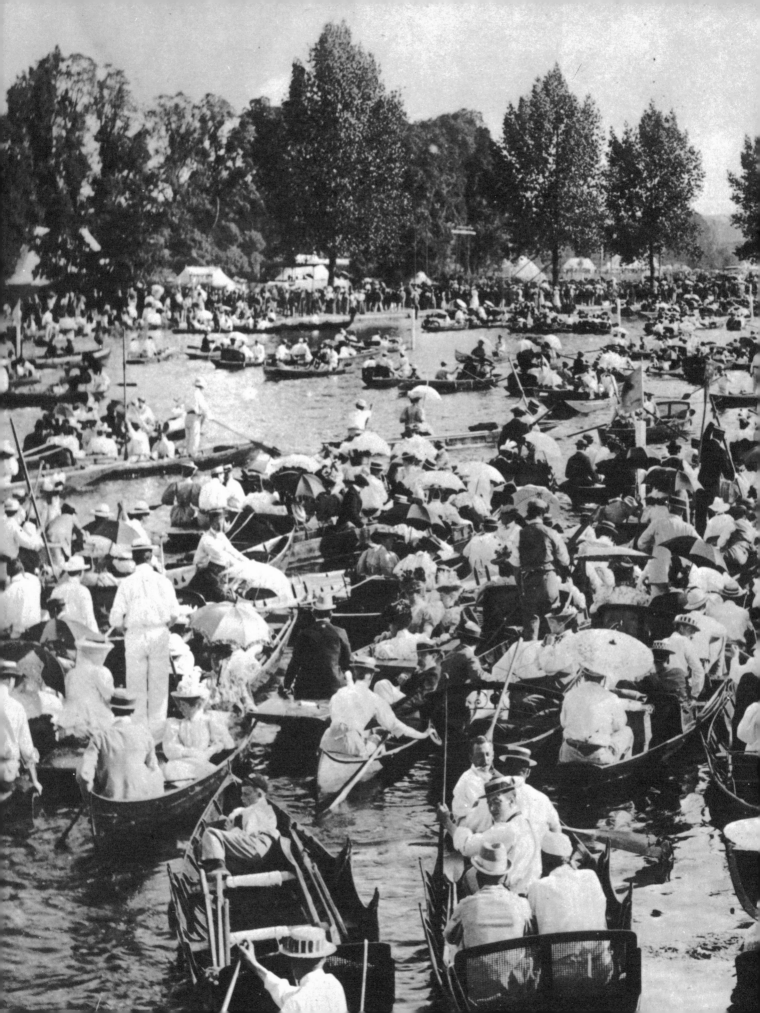

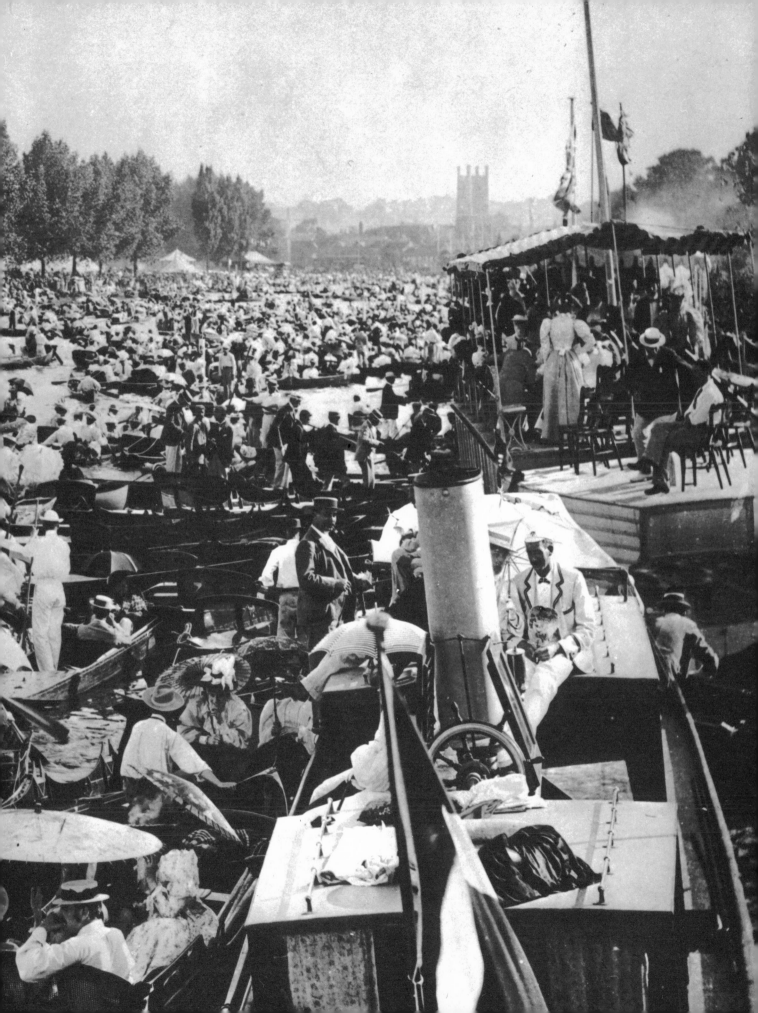

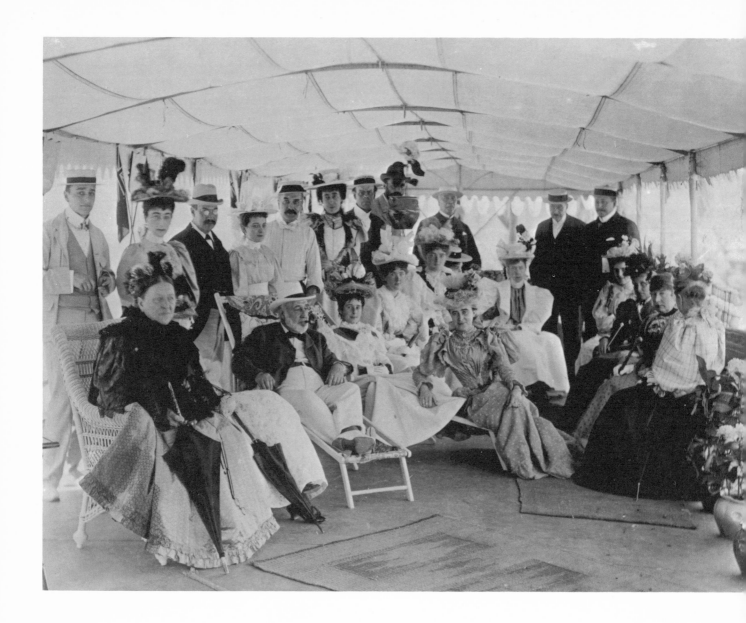

34 A group of splendid sartorial elegance aboard the houseboat *Stella*, during Henley week in the 1890s. The Regatta – established in 1839 and held at the beginning of July – was the great event of the season, on a par with Ascot and Goodwood.

35 The falling weir-terraces of the middle reaches of the Thames are one of the river's most graceful sights. This photograph shows the nineteenth-century Gothic church at Marlow, taken from the weir, *c.* 1900.

36 Loading logs on to a Thames barge, *c.* 1885; they were probably felled in nearby Quarry Woods. In the background is Marlow suspension bridge erected in 1835, to replace the old wooden pile bridge. It is associated with the story of 'puppy pie' which was supposedly stolen from a near-by inn by an unscrupulous bargee, and was frequently quoted as a reproach to his successors.

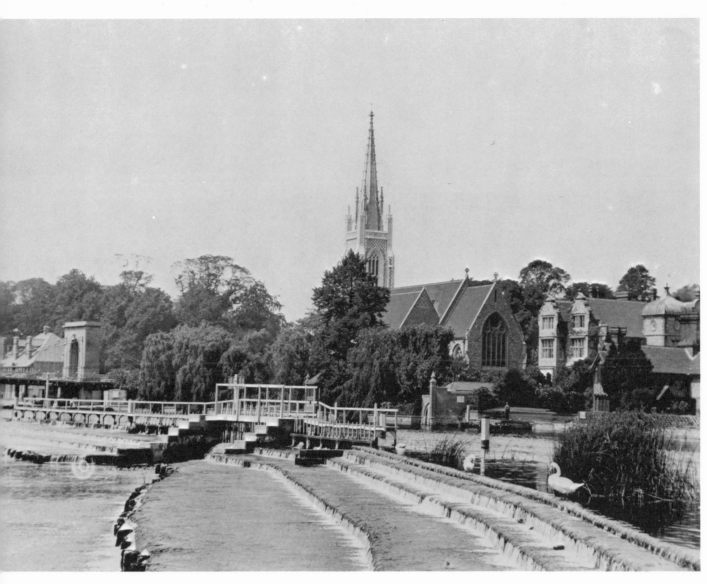

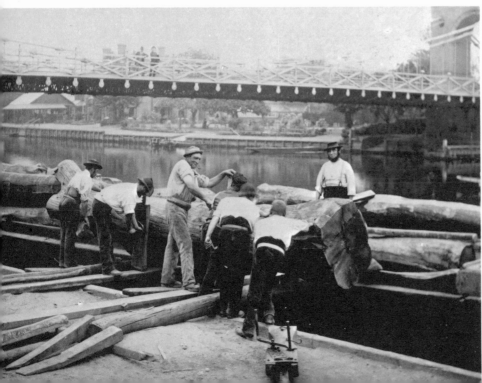

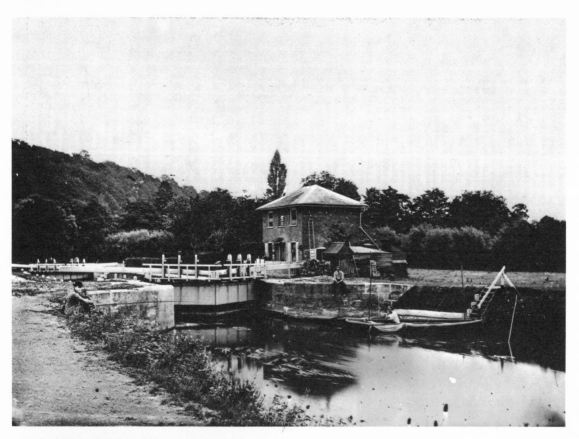

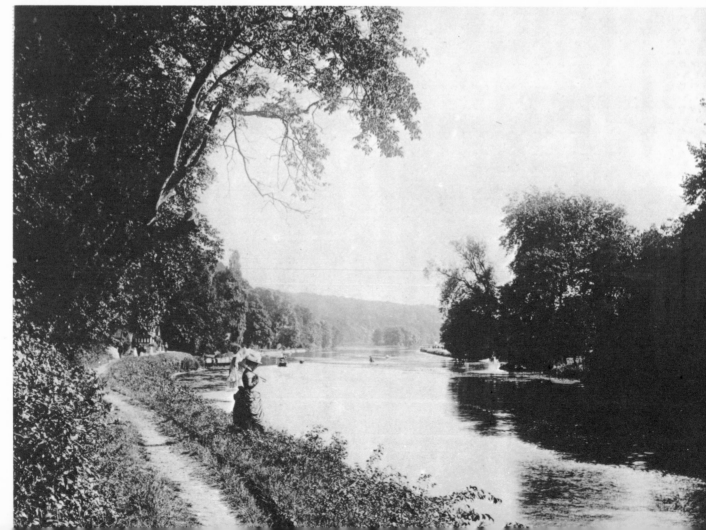

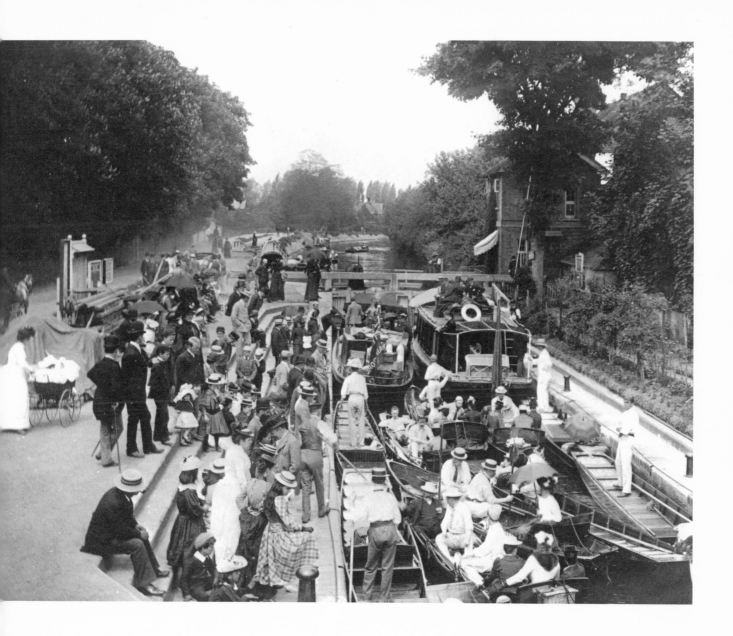

37   Cookham lock, *c.* 1865: the most beautifully situated lock on the river, with the woods of Hedsor and Cliveden rising above. A popular haunt for fishermen, who readily caught the now elusive Thames trout.

38   Hedsor near Cliveden Reach, one of the most picturesque stretches of the Thames. A pretty young woman with bustle and parasol contemplates her reflection from the towing path, *c.* 1885.

39   Boulter's lock on an August bank holiday weekend with a crowd of small boats, *c.* 1895. It was usually the busiest lock on the river and, on such an occasion as this, more than twenty boats with a steam-launch or two would be crammed through.

> It was a glorious day, and the lock was crowded; and, as is a common practice up the river, a speculative photographer was taking a picture of us all as we lay upon the rising waters.
> . . . Everybody in the lock seemed to have been suddenly struck wooden. They were all standing or sitting about in the most quaint and curious attitudes I have ever seen off a Japanese fan. All the girls were smiling. Oh, they did look so sweet! And all the fellows were frowning, and looking stern and noble.

Jerome K. Jerome, *Three Men in a Boat,* 1889.

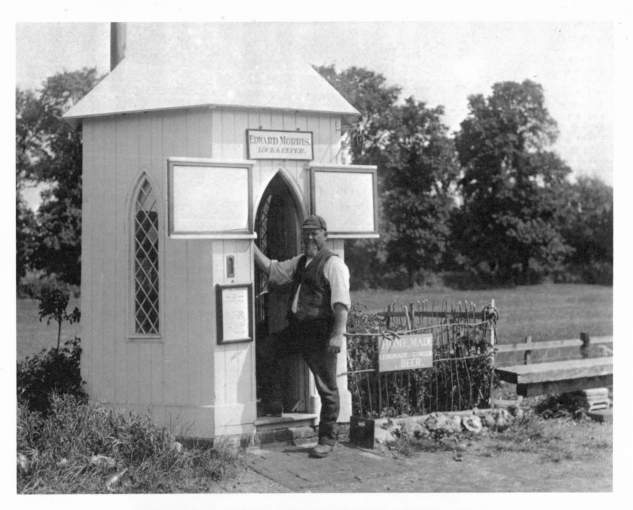

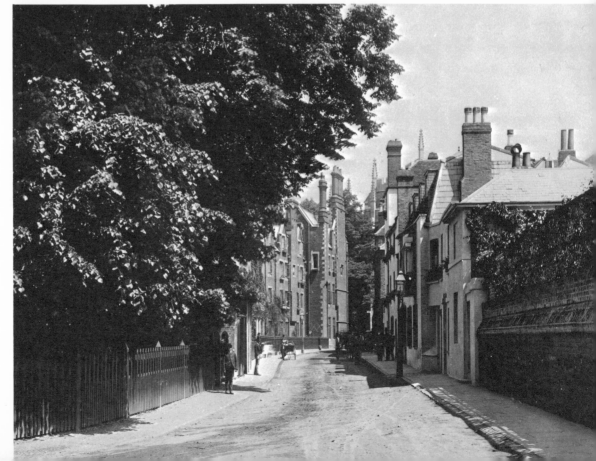

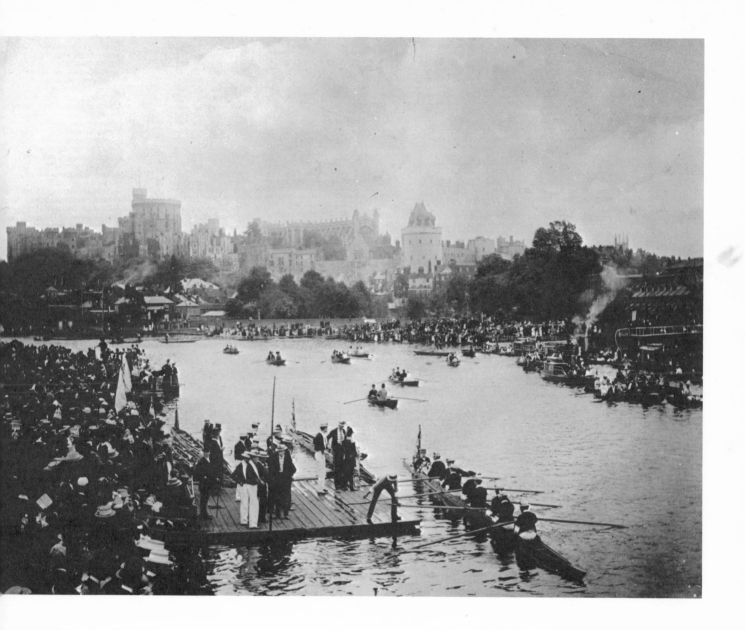

40   The lock-keeper at Bray, Edward Morris, *c.* 1890.
Morris was one of the working-men of the Thames with
whom Taunt 'chummed' for many years.

41   Eton College, Buckinghamshire, *c.* 1890, showing
Keate's Lane. The pinnacles of the college chapel appear
in the background whilst the buildings in the foreground
are boys' boarding houses. On the right 'Evans's', far left
'Hawtrey House', near left 'Coleridge House' and,
obscured by the tree, 'Keate House'. 'Coleridge House'
was demolished in 1938 but the other three are still
standing today.

42   The annual Eton boating regatta on the Windsor
stretch of the river in 1888. It was instituted to
commemorate a visit of George III, and is held each year
on his birthday, 4 June. The event, which is now held
on the weir stream at Romney, gives the name to
'Fireworks Eyot', after the evening festivities.

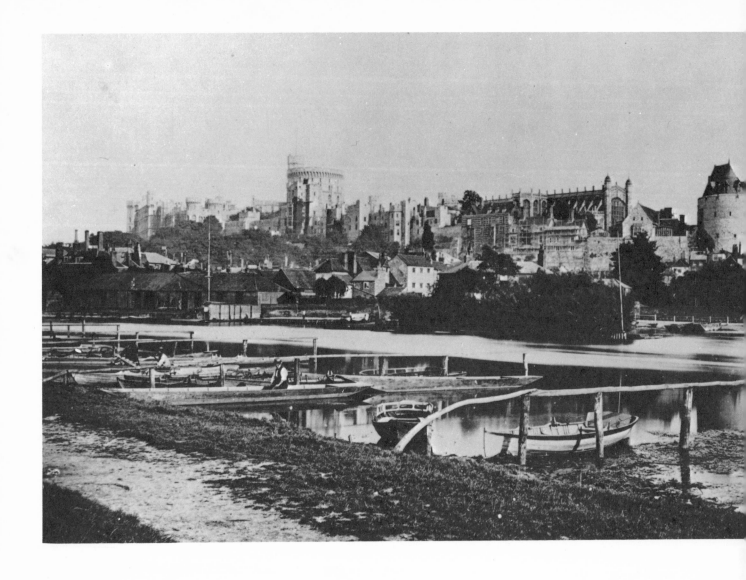

43 An early Taunt view of Windsor Castle, taken from the Brocas meadow in 1865.

44 A favourite place for river outings, the Picnic at Ankerwycke, shaded by lime trees. It was burnt down in the 1930s. It is traditionally believed to have been the meeting-place of Henry VIII and Anne Boleyn; he is said to have waited here for the signal announcing her execution at Tower Hill.

45 An early picture taken at Bell Weir in 1863 shows clearly the intricate arrangement of rymers and paddles of the old weir.

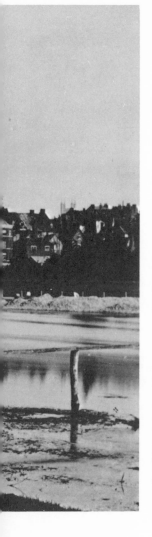
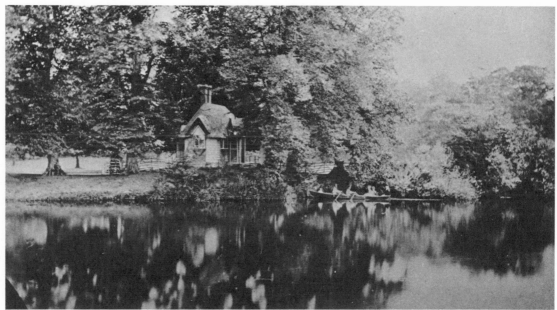
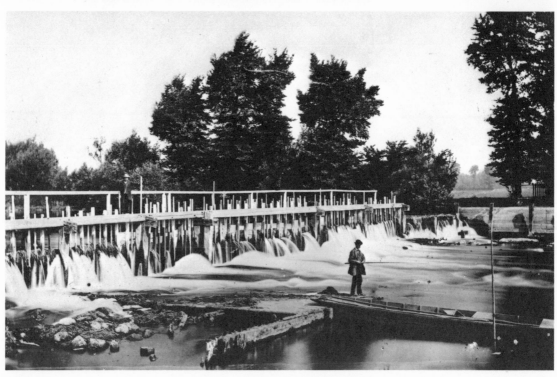

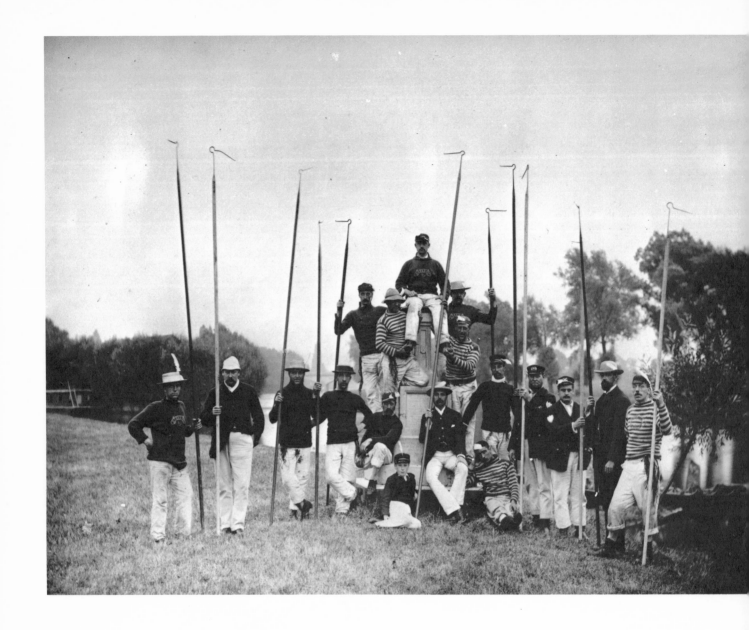

46 The Swan-Uppers on the London Stone at Staines in 1888. This annual event, which still takes place, is the ancient rite of marking the swans. The swan-owning London livery companies, the Dyers and Vintners, and the Swan Masters of the Crown exercise their rights each July. Shown here are the Dyers who bumped their new hands next to the London Stone to allow them freedom of the river.

47 Abbey Mill, Chertsey, taken about 1865, a picturesque wooden structure with quaint out-buildings; it stood on a site previously built upon by the Benedictine monks, and has now disappeared.

48 Molesey boat-slide at the lock in the late 1880s.

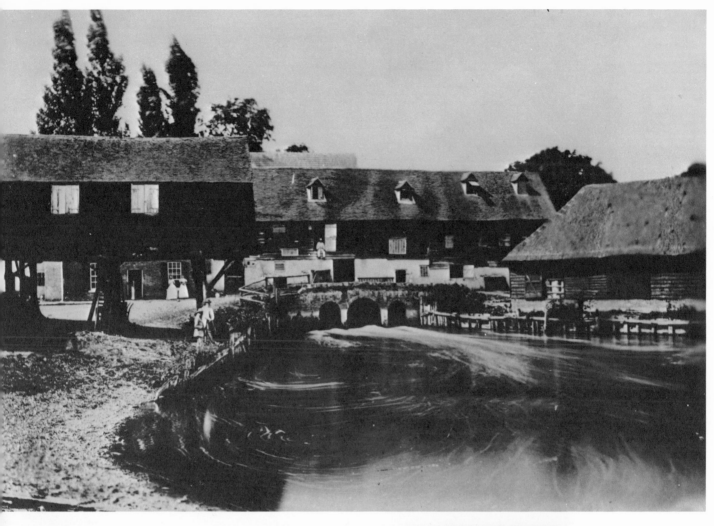

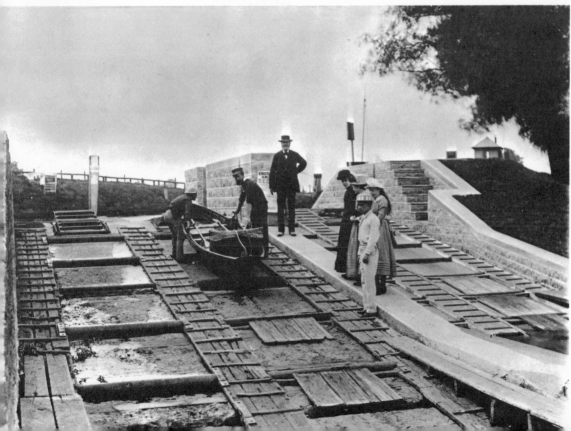

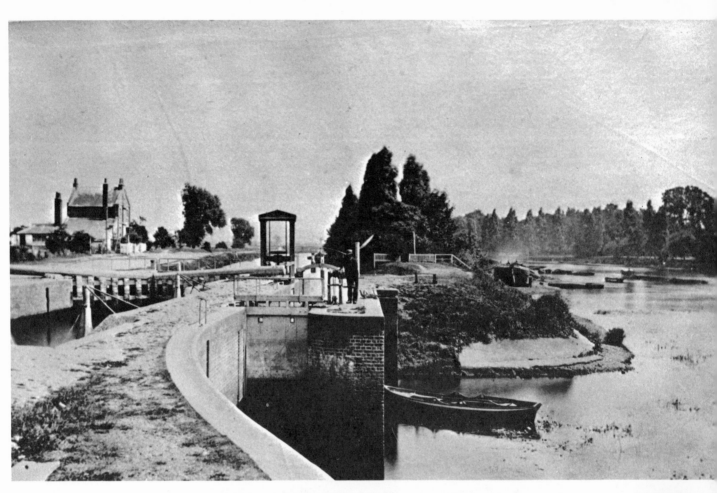

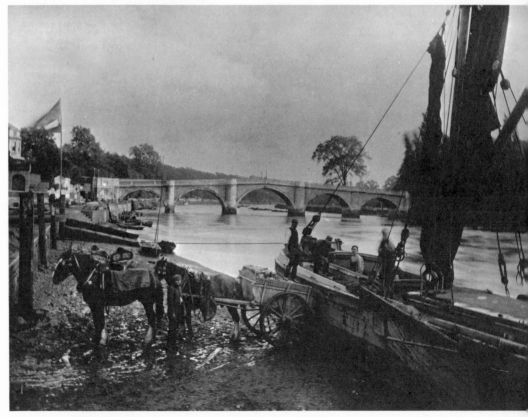

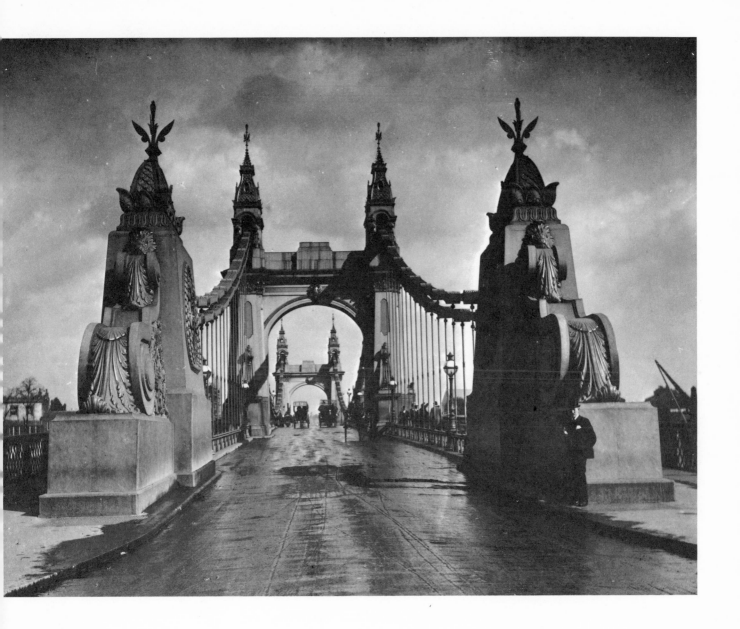

49 Teddington lock and weir, *c.* 1870: the last and also
the largest lock on the river.

50 A group of men unloading bricks, probably from the
east coast, with horses standing on the hard near
Richmond Bridge, *c.* 1896.

51 Hammersmith Bridge, *c.* 1895: a monumental
Victorian structure built in 1884–5. The gentleman in top
hat and monocle is as characteristic of the age as the
design of the bridge.

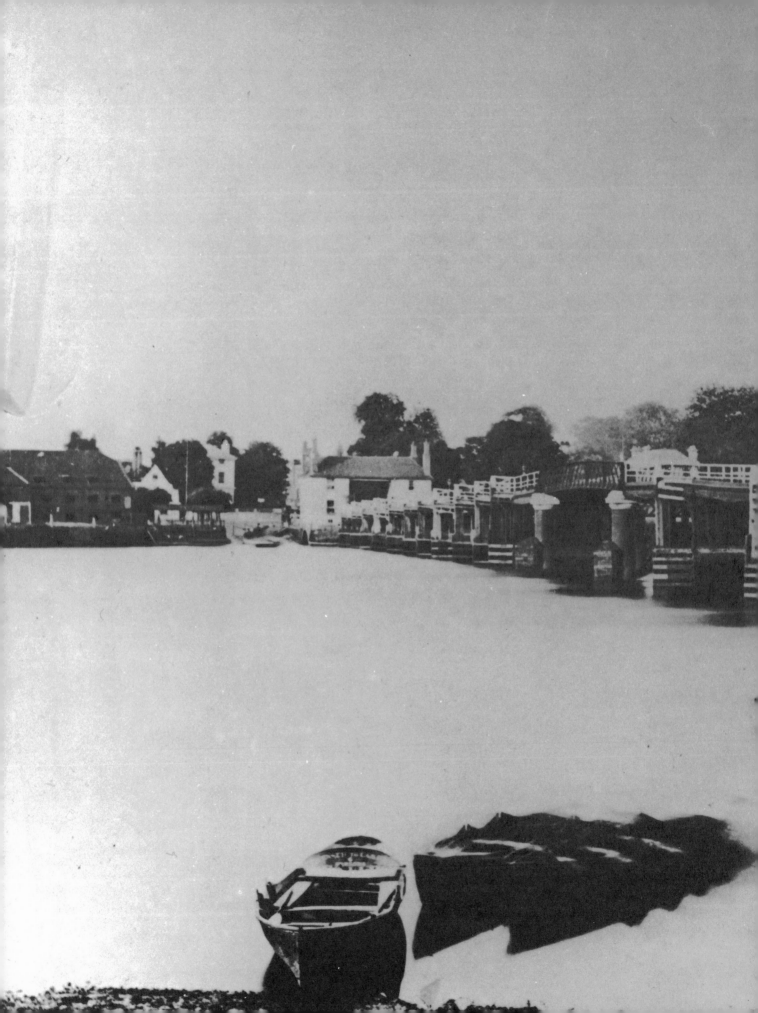

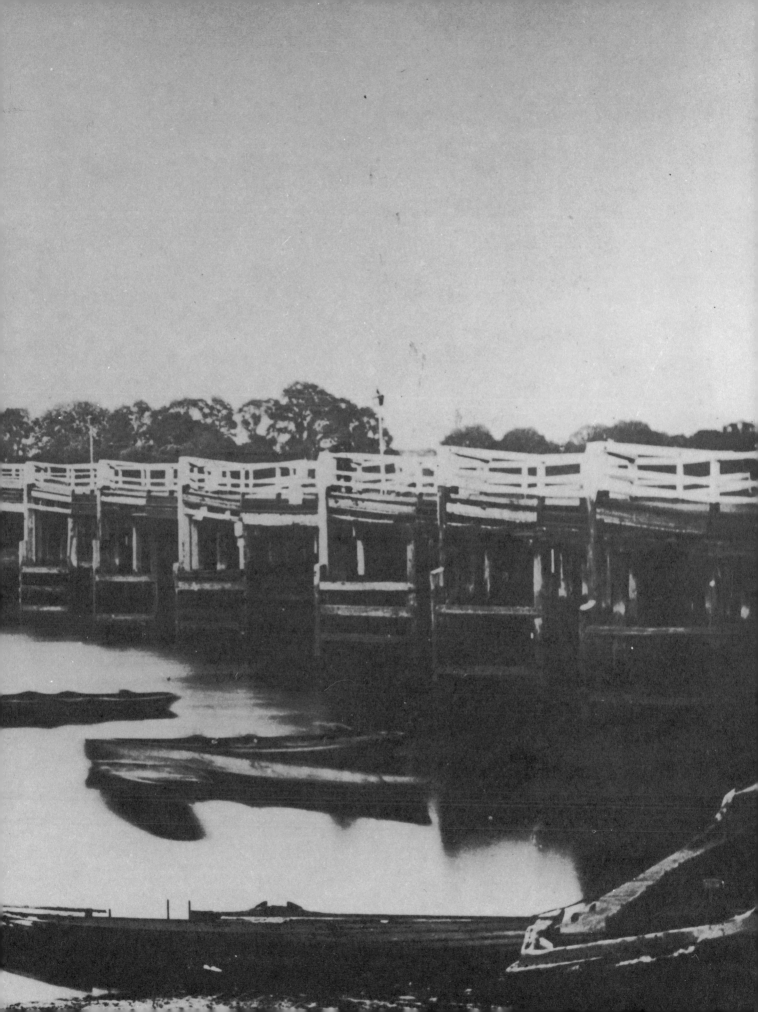

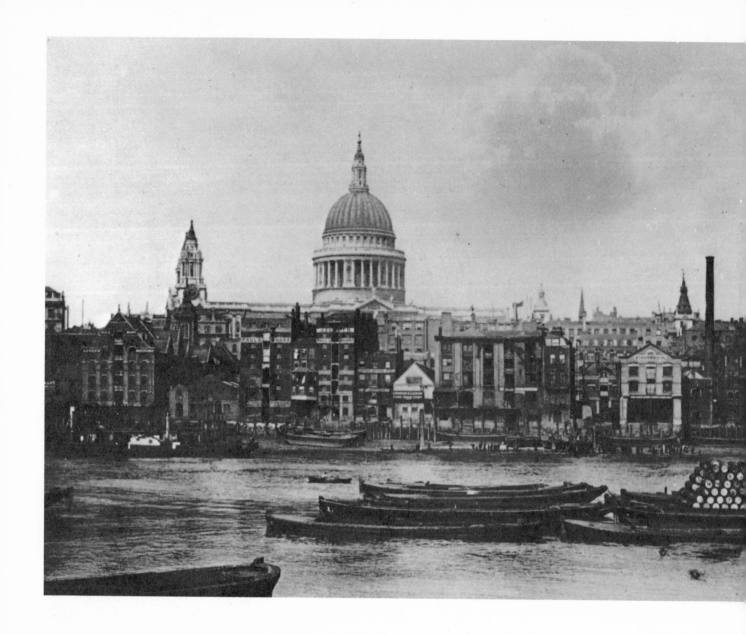

52 *previous page* Old Putney Bridge was the last of the
wooden structures which formerly spanned the Thames.
This bridge, completed in 1729, was removed in 1886 for
the new granite bridge designed by Sir Joseph Bazalgette.
It is interesting to contemplate the rural scene which was
Putney just over one hundred years ago.

53 St Paul's, *c.* 1880; photographed from a position
near to Wren's house in Southwark, from which he
studied the development of his masterpiece.

54 London seems to have had traffic problems in the
last century comparable with those of today. This
photograph shows London Bridge in the 1880s, laden
with goods vehicles coming up from the country.

55 A peep under London Bridge, *c.* 1865.

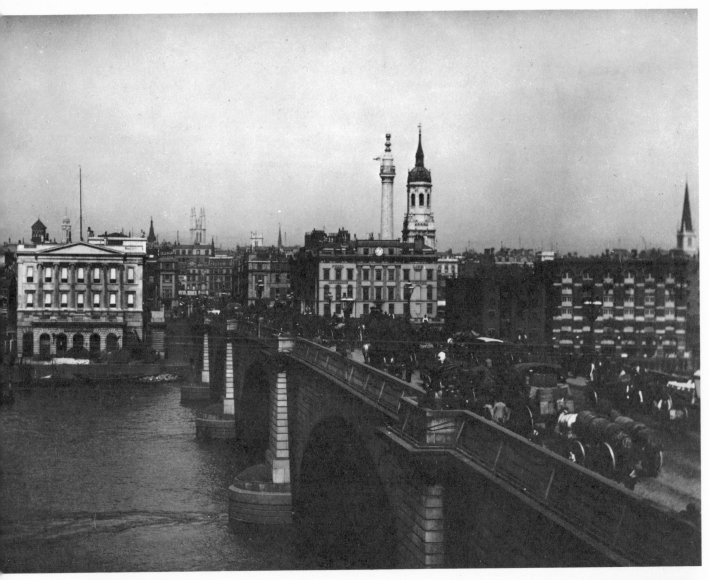

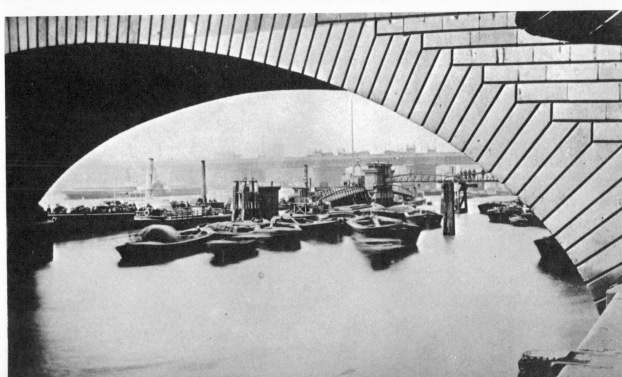

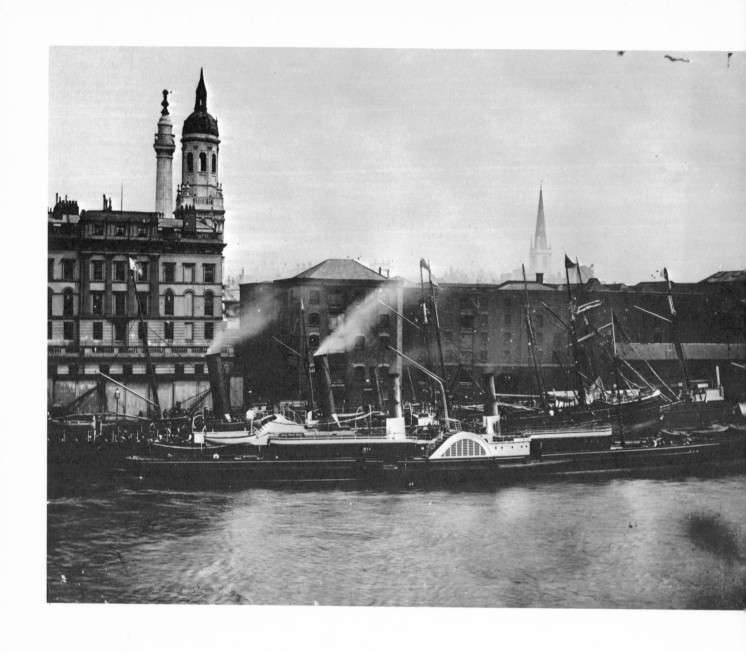

56   An early-paddle steamer, *Princess Alice*, at Swan Steps, London Bridge, perhaps bound for Margate or Southend, *c*. 1870.

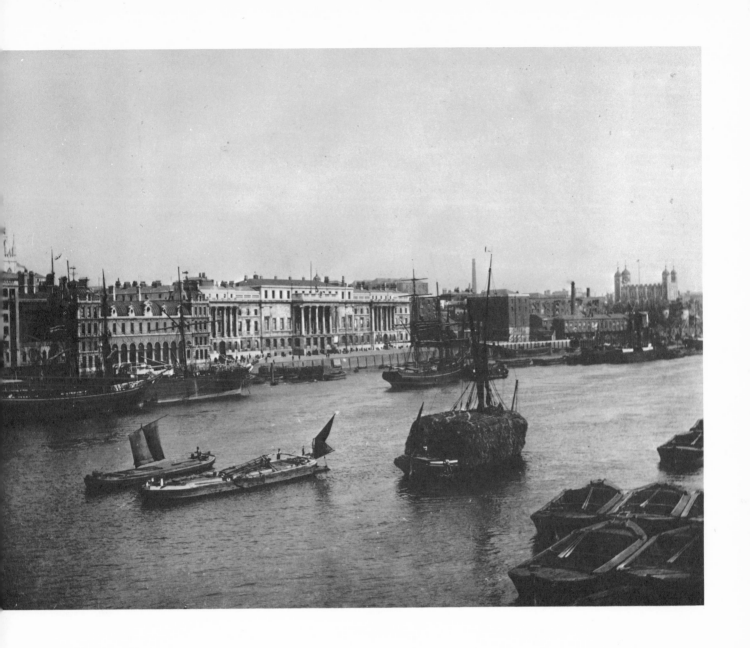

57   The Thames with hayboat, looking towards Customs House and the Tower of London, taken from London Bridge, *c.* 1880.

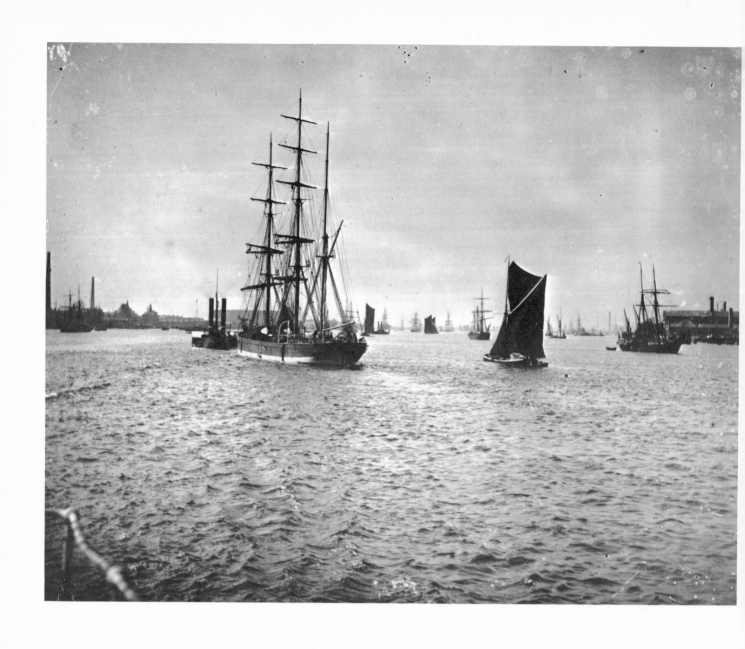

58 The Lower Thames, *c.* 1880, with towing barque and barge, probably near Limehouse. A barque is a two- or three-masted vessel with fore and main masts square rigged and a barge is a flat-bottomed freight boat with or without sails.

Oxford

Oxford was Taunt's place of birth, the city where he lived his long life and his continual source of inspiration. His photographs of Oxford capture the beauty of its medieval townscape before the onslaught of the twentieth century, and represent some of his most accomplished architectural work. For this record we owe him a great debt. His photographs evoke the qualities which, to those who love Oxford, are unforgettable, but they are qualities which, alas, are fast disappearing. For all time, he has captured the streets in moods of tranquillity and festivity, the river as a place of work and enjoyment and the characteristics of both the University and the market town.

Every provincial city has, at different times, its notable personalities. Oxford had Henry W. Taunt. A lifelong supporter of all the traditional Oxford events – May Day, Eights Week, Beating the Bounds, St Giles Fair – he was ever present. He must have been a remarkable sight with his long white beard, dressed in knickerbockers and with a wild flower in his buttonhole, nearly always the small white pimpernel rose. On river days he would be seen in reefer jacket and yachting cap, selling his wares or taking photographs. He is well remembered during Eights Weeks for his yellow cameras mounted on large wooden tripods at strategic points along the towing-path, so that he could record the races at every stage (Plate 78).

As well as photographing Oxford, Henry Taunt translated his love of the town into much well-documented written work; he probably knew as much of Oxford's history and architecture as any of his contemporaries, if not more.

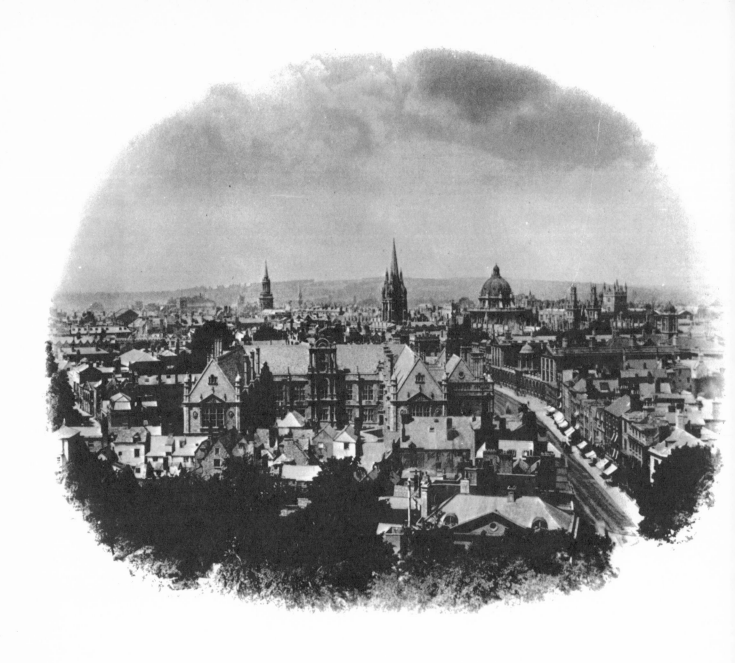

59 From Magdalen Tower, looking up the High, *c.* 1900. The city is seen as a glorious panorama. The Examination Schools, Radcliffe Camera, and the spires of St Mary and of All Saints are the principal features, while the Wytham hills form a delightful background.

60 Christ Church, *c.* 1880. showing Tom Tower which was completed by Sir Christopher Wren, from the east side of Tom Quad.

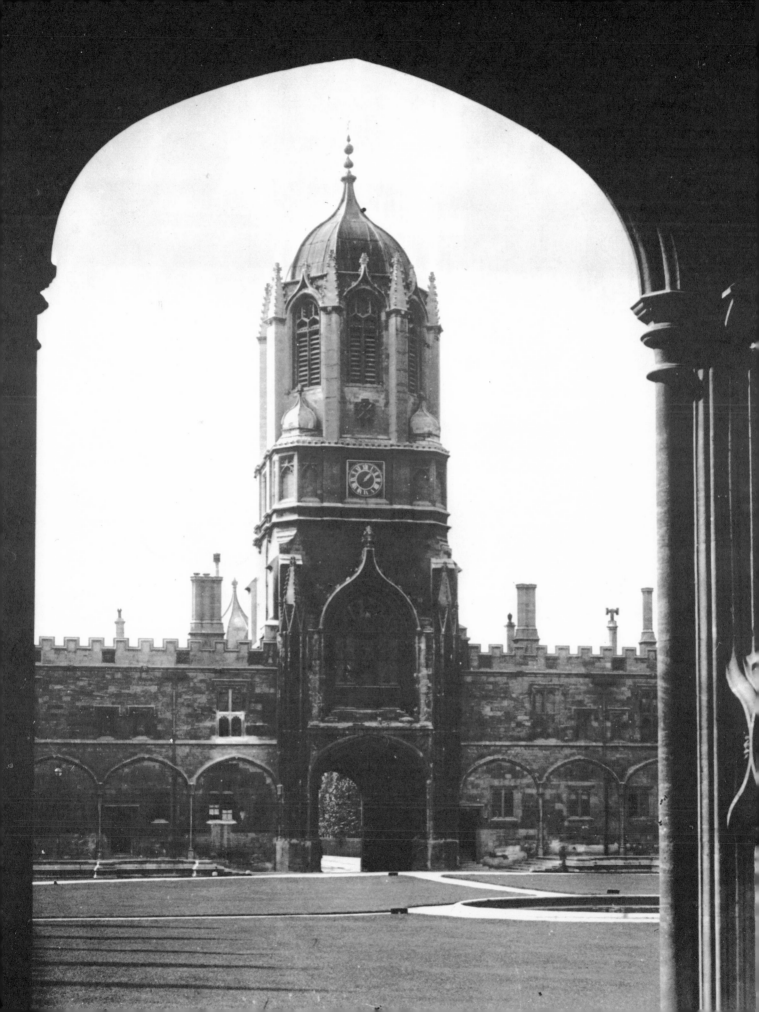

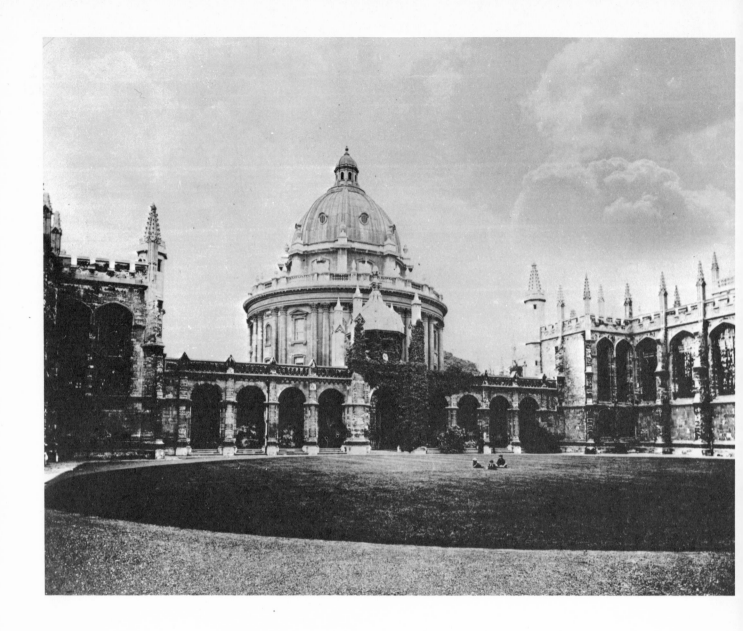

61   The Radcliffe Camera from All Souls quadrangle,
c. 1870. Designed by James Gibbs, England's first example
of a round library was opened in 1749.

62   One of the finest streets in the world, Oxford High
in 1897. Left, University College; centre, St Mary's
Church; beyond, All Souls College; right, the Queen's
College.

63   A stereoscopic view of St Mary the Virgin Church,
c. 1870. The porch of the University church is a fine
example of English Baroque and an interesting illustration
of how contrasting architectural styles can blend.

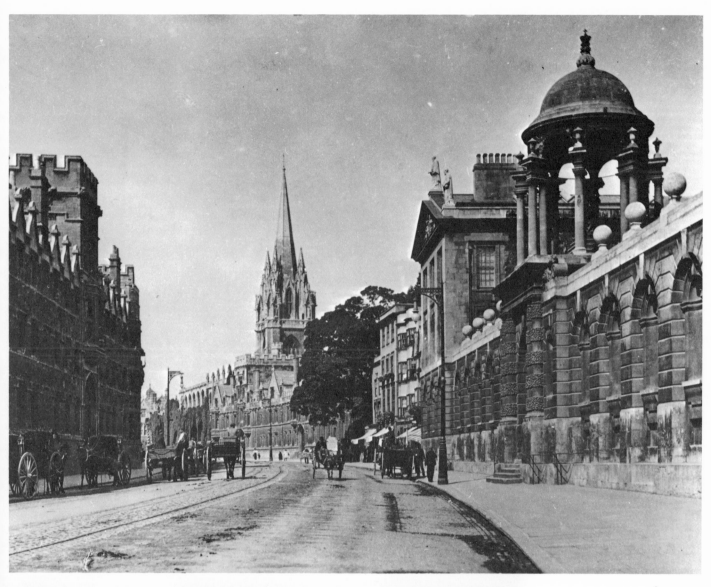

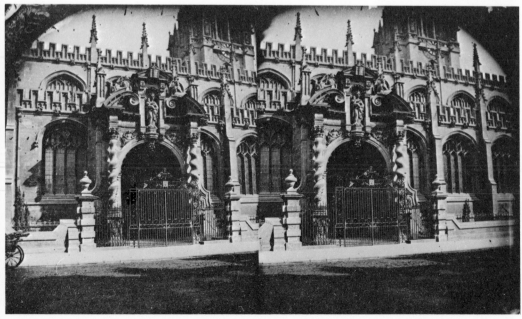

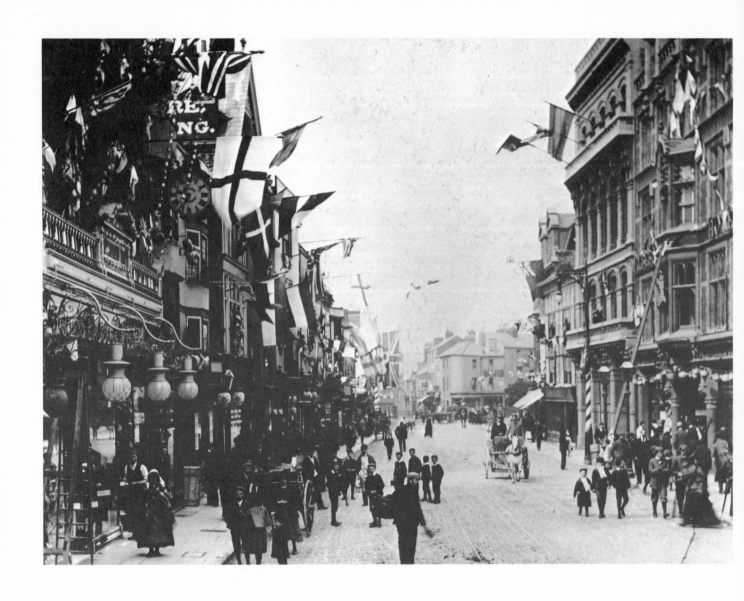

64 Queen Street, looking west, at the time of the
Diamond Jubilee celebrations in 1897. This street is very
different today, the West Gate development having
replaced the buildings in the background.

65 Cornmarket Street from Carfax, with a horse-drawn
tram of the Oxford Tramways Company in August 1907.
The façades and shop fronts are now very much changed.

66 The Golden Cross Hotel, Cornmarket, with an early
motor-car replacing the coaching horses in the courtyard,
c. 1907. It has been an inn since about 1200 but since
1970 only provides food.

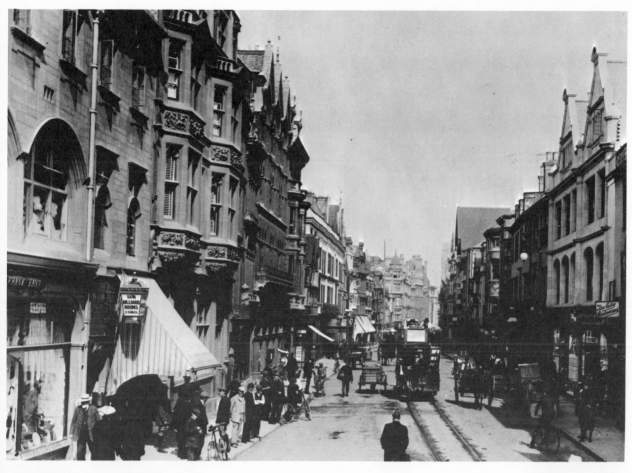

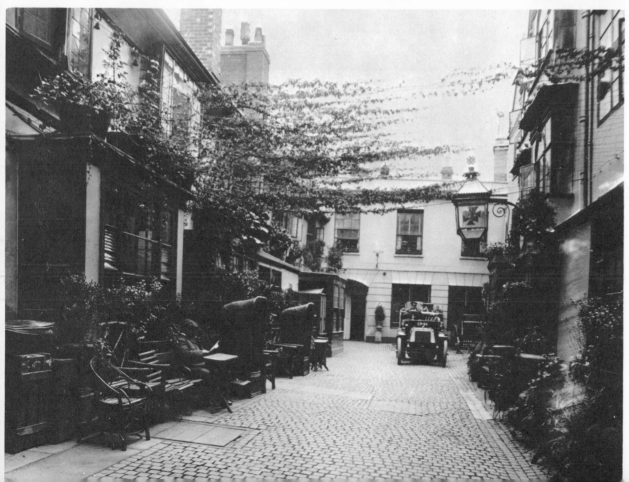

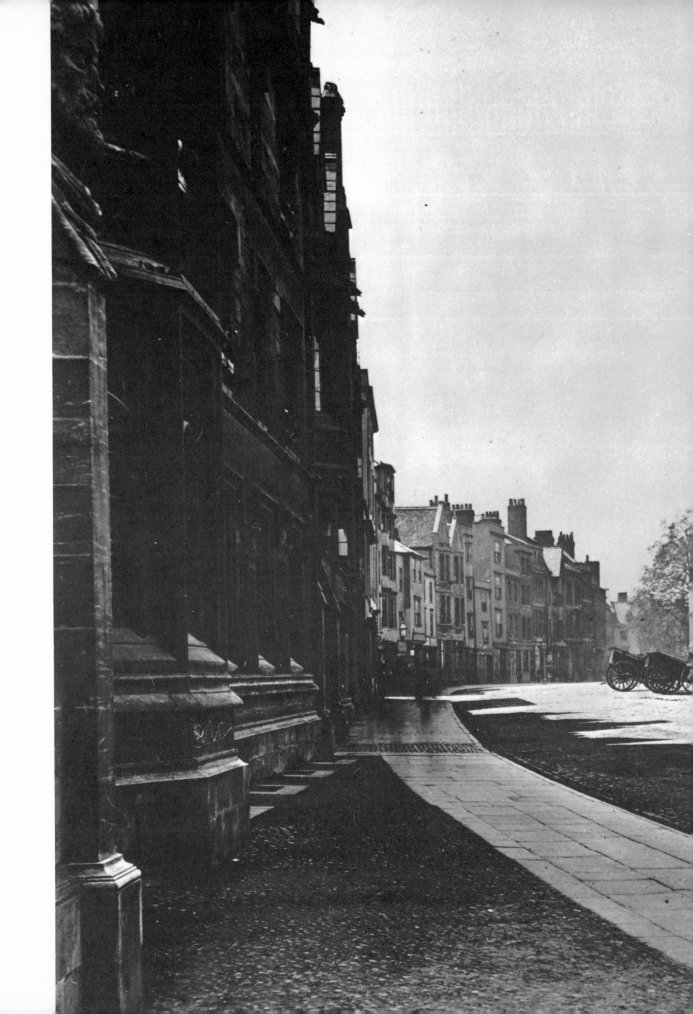

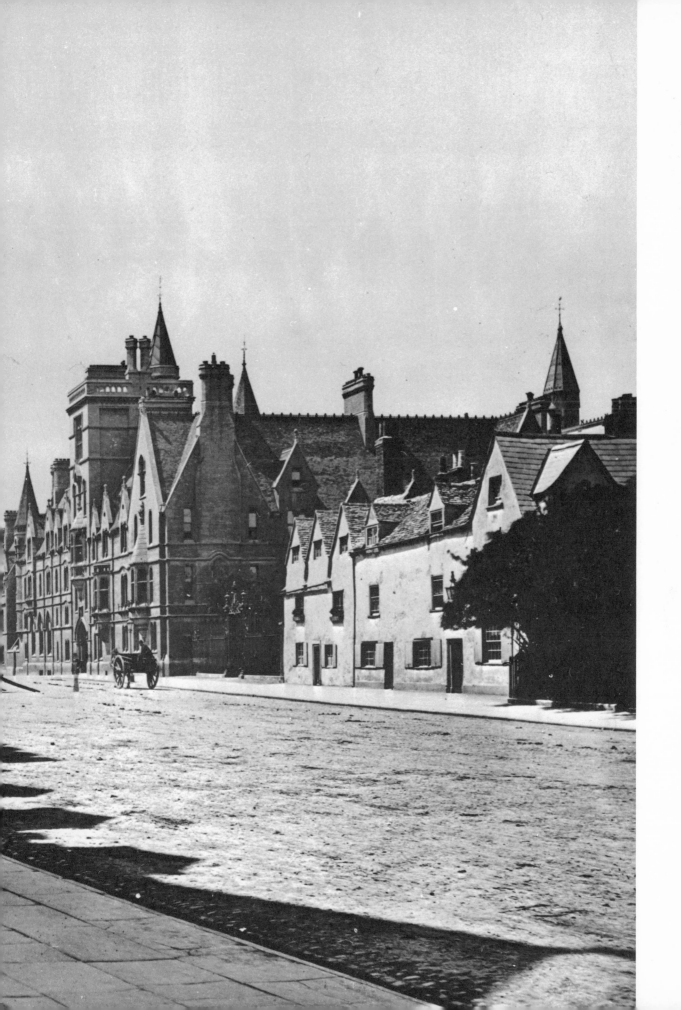

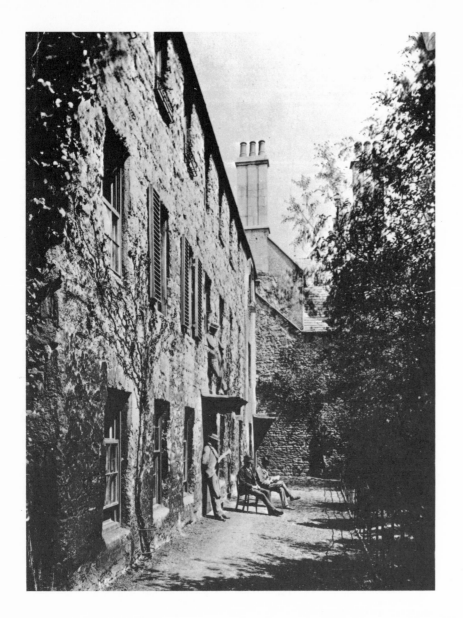

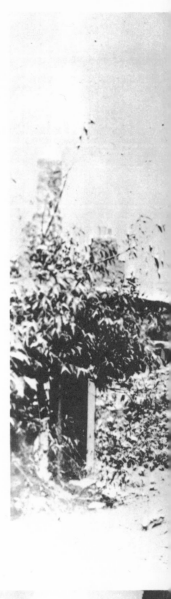

67 *previous page* A tranquil scene: Broad Street, photographed from the south, *c.* 1870, showing on the nearside the façade of Exeter College and on the far side the old houses belonging to Trinity College which have recently been renovated.

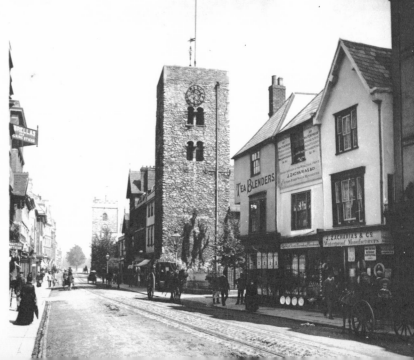

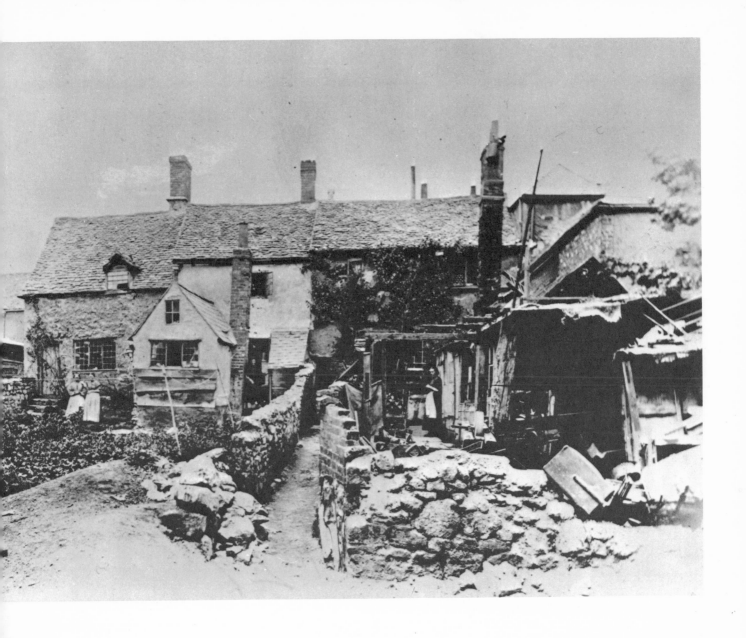

68   University undergraduates lazing in the sun,
Lincoln College Grove, *c.* 1870.

69   The oldest building in the city, the eleventh-century
tower of St Michael-at-the-Northgate, dominates the
peaceful view of Cornmarket Street, *c.* 1880.

70   Old houses in George Street, *c.* 1875. This is the site
of the City of Oxford High School which is now an
annexe to the College of Further Education.

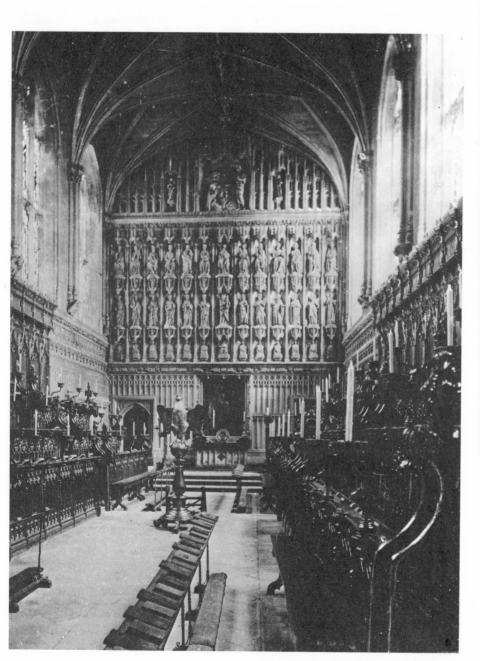
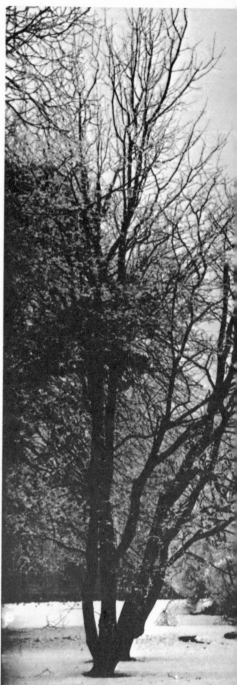

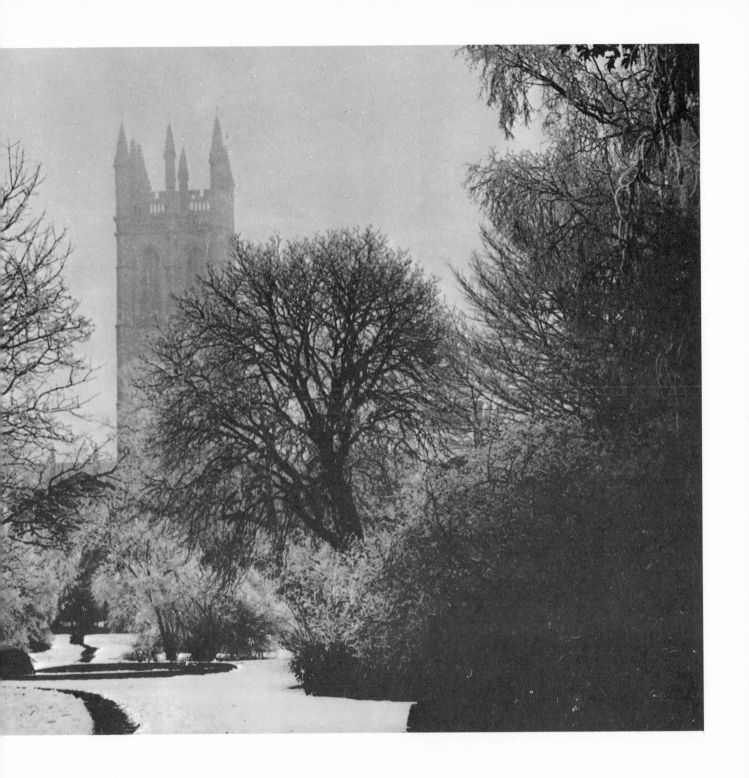

71 Magdalen College Chapel looking east, *c.* 1875. The reredos was completed in 1866 after the niches had been left empty since 1828–9 when L. N. Cottingham redesigned the interior.

72 A well-known Oxford landmark, Magdalen Tower, and the Botanical Gardens in winter, *c.* 1880.

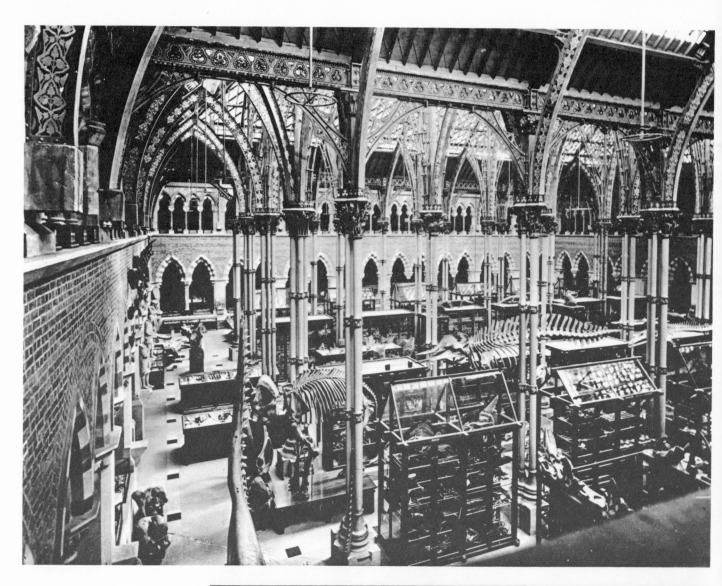

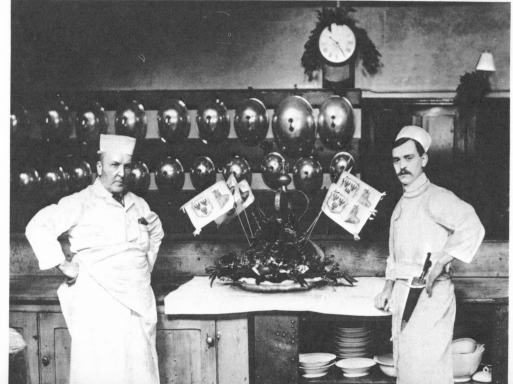

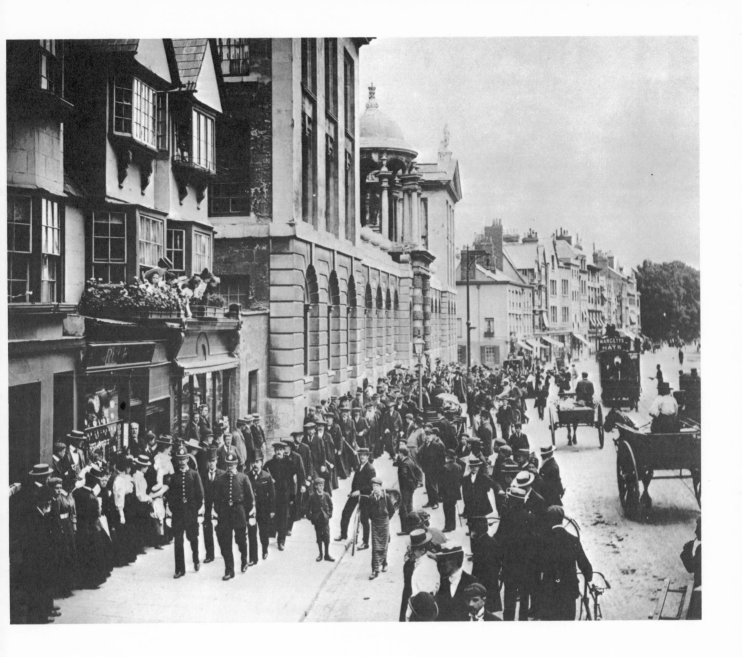

73   The interior of the University Museum from the north-east in 1870. The photograph shows the ornamental ironwork in Victorian Gothic style by Skidmore of Coventry.

74   The Boar's Head prepared for the annual festivity at the Queen's College on Christmas Day 1902. This is a survival of an old baronial custom. In the nineteenth century crowds of visitors came to the College to witness the ceremony.

75   An Encaenia procession of the University in 1897 in the High, being led by Vice-Chancellor Magrath of Queen's and Chief Constable Oswald Cole.

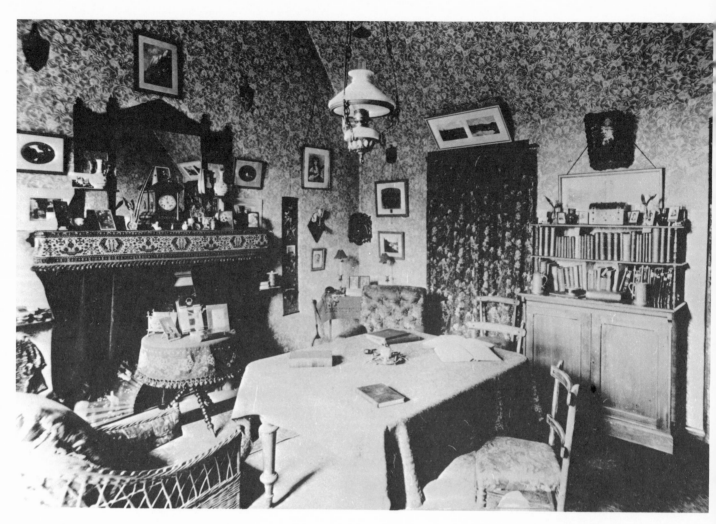

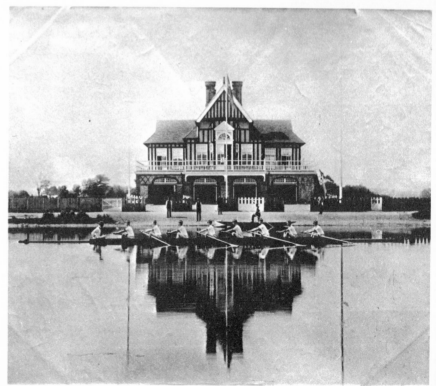

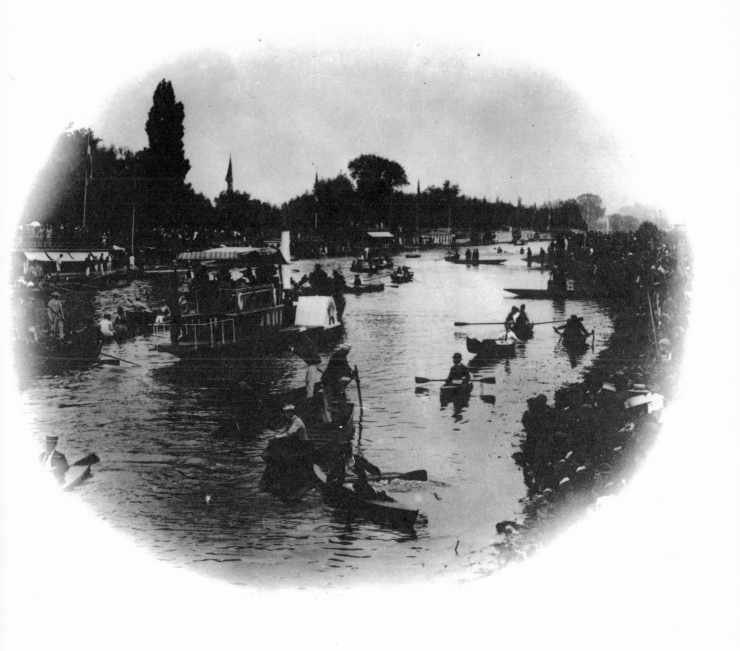

76 A glimpse of a typical undergraduate's room in the 1890s.

77 An early photograph of a college eight, sitting in theatrical style, on the Isis at the Oxford University boat-house, with the boat-house staff grouped in the background, c. 1865.

78 A paddle-steamer going through the boats at Eights Week in 1889. On the right, one of Taunt's assistants with tripod can be seen ready to secure views of the racing.

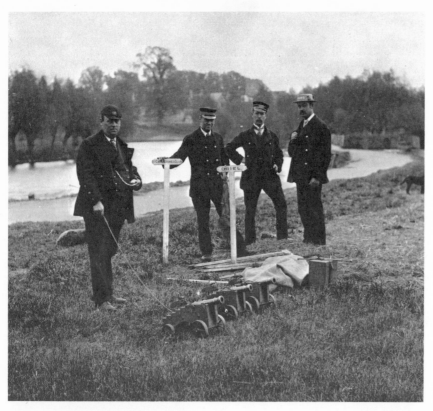

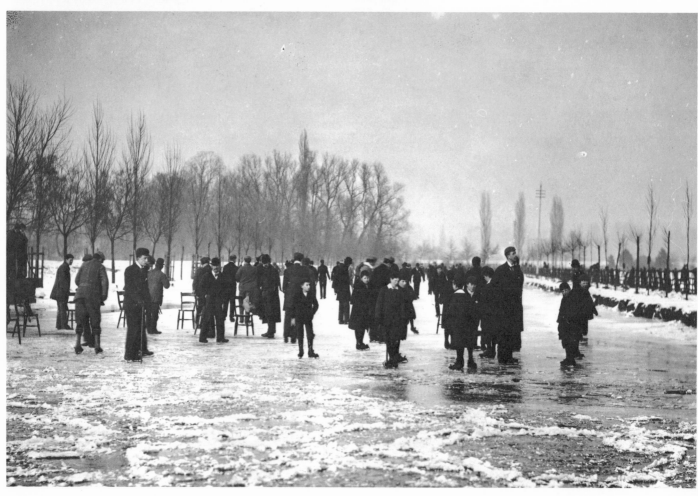

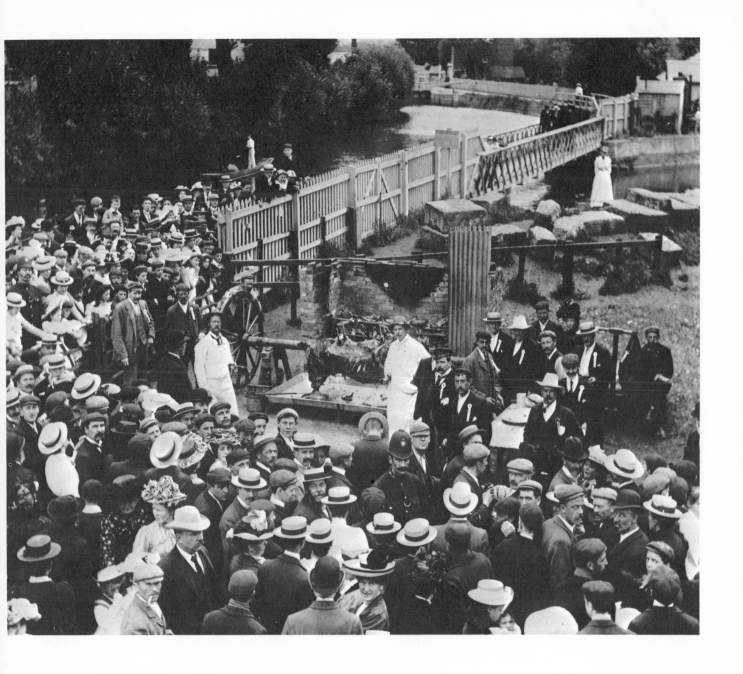

79 Tims the timekeeper and starter at the Oxford
Eights, showing off his starting cannons, time-piece and
assistants, *c.* 1910.

80 Skating on the Cherwell Cut, February 1895. The
cut was made in 1883, through Christ Church Meadow.

81 A Jubilee ox-roast at Osney by the Thames, in
June 1887.

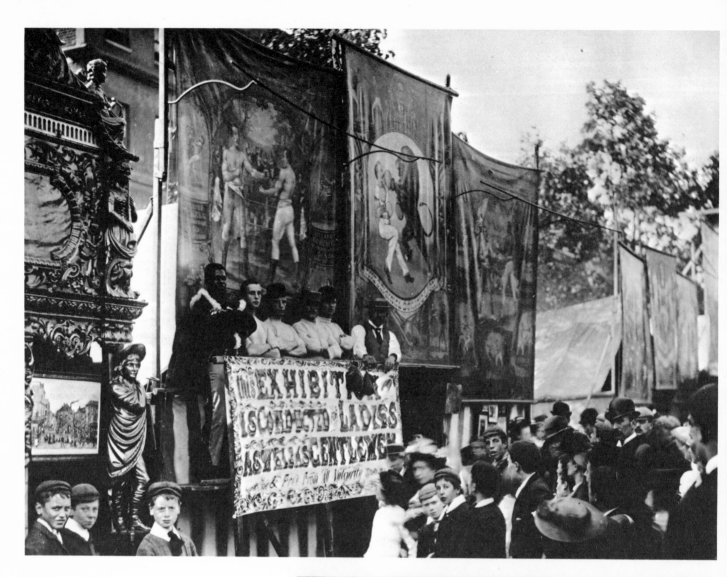

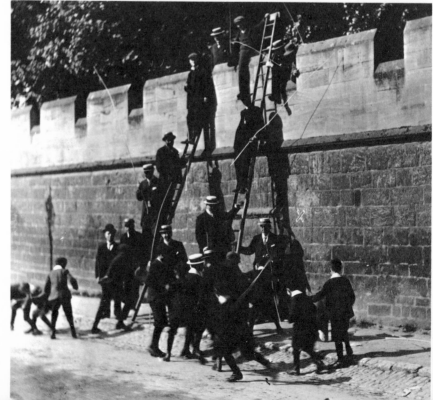

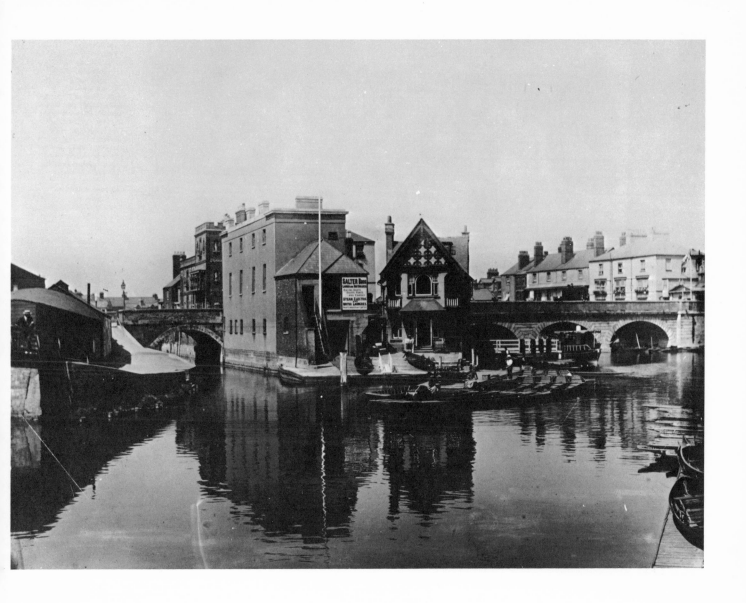

82   The Boxing Booth at St Giles' Fair in 1898. The
poster on the front reads: 'This exhibition is conducted
for ladies as well as gentlemen and is free from all
vulgarity.'

83   Beating the Bounds at Longwall in May 1908. The
enthusiastic choirboys are scrambling for coins.

84   Salter's Boatyard and Folly Bridge from the river in
1911. It is from here that the famous Oxford & Kingston
steamer service runs.

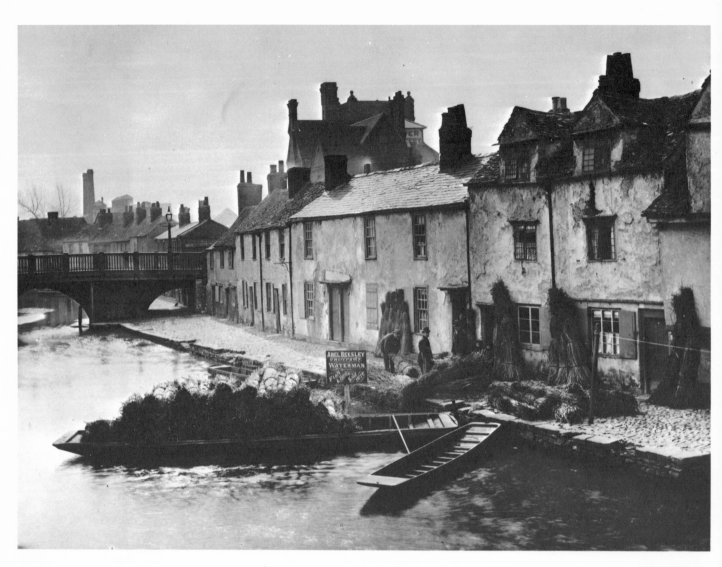

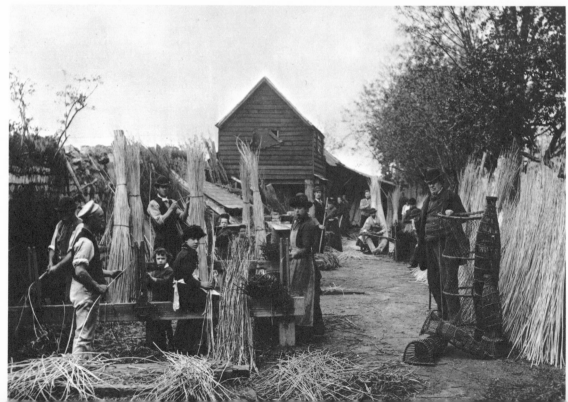

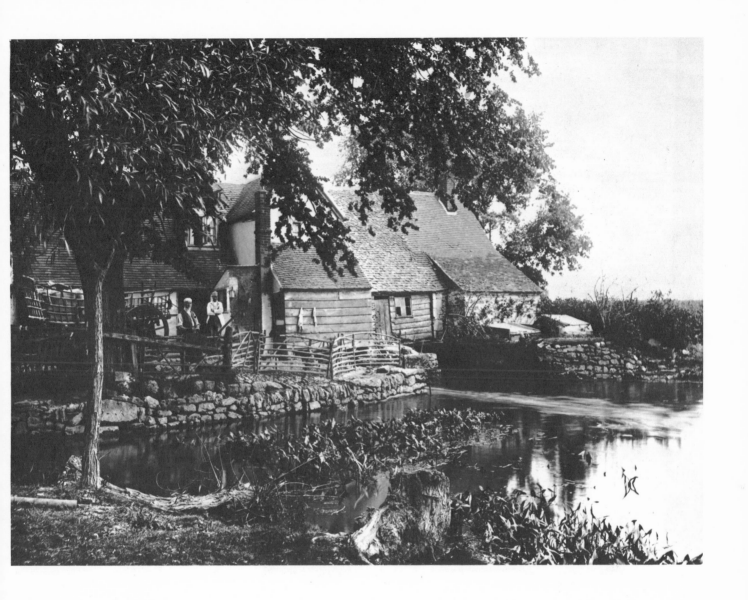

85   Abel Beesley, the University waterman, with his rush
punt at Fisher Row in October 1900.

86   Osier peeling, making eel traps and crayfish creels at
Beesley's yard near Hythe Bridge in April 1900.

87   Botley Corn Mill about 1875; after a long and
interesting history, the mill was demolished in 1923 for
road-widening purposes.

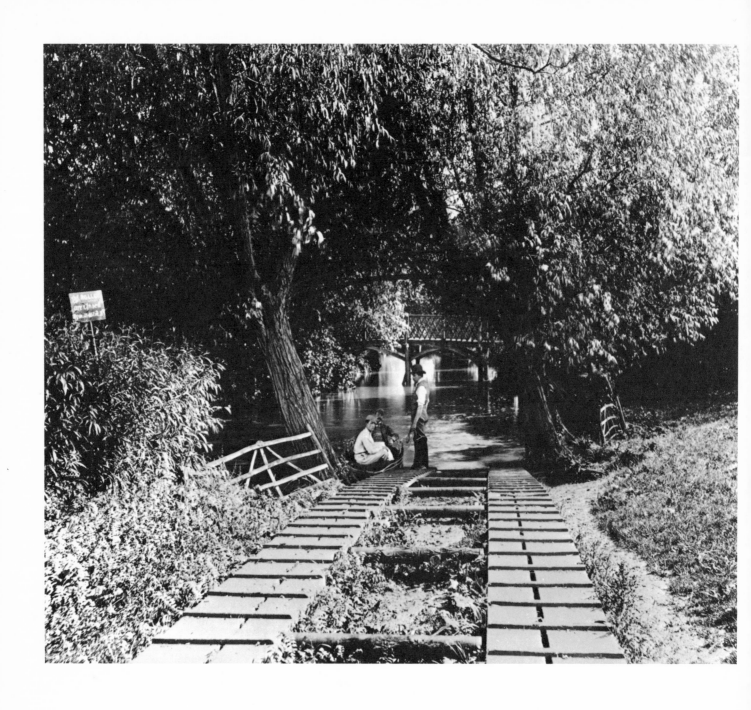

88   The Rollers at Parson's Pleasure, Mesopotamia, *c.* 1885. This is the place where ladies still have to disembark on their punting trips up the Cherwell to save their blushes, lest they pass the bathing place where men bathe naked.

Taunt's Home Counties

The majority of Taunt's work was done in his home counties, those of Oxfordshire, Berkshire and Buckinghamshire, the countryside immortalized in the last century by the poetry of Matthew Arnold and the delightful books of Flora Thompson, *Lark Rise to Candleford* and *Still Glides the Stream*. It was to the towns, villages and hamlets of these three counties that Taunt could most easily travel by his limited means of transport. I have related in my introduction how Taunt first became familiar with the countryside at West Ilsley in the Berkshire Downs, his mother's home, and how in later years he became a familiar entertainer in many town and village halls. His love of natural things is evident from his work and frequently in later years when business pressures increased he sought sanctuary in the ordered and peaceful existence of rural life.

His work in these counties was to record the splendour of the many fine houses and churches, and the way of life of the people. Taunt took his pictures from scenes that had survived without change for many hundreds of years; but were to change radically after August 1914. He shows us situations which today seem almost unbelievable, village streets overrun with horses, sheep and cattle and enthusiastic street celebrations – an age in which the streets with their varied and lively activities filled a far more important social role than do today's busy and noisy thoroughfares.

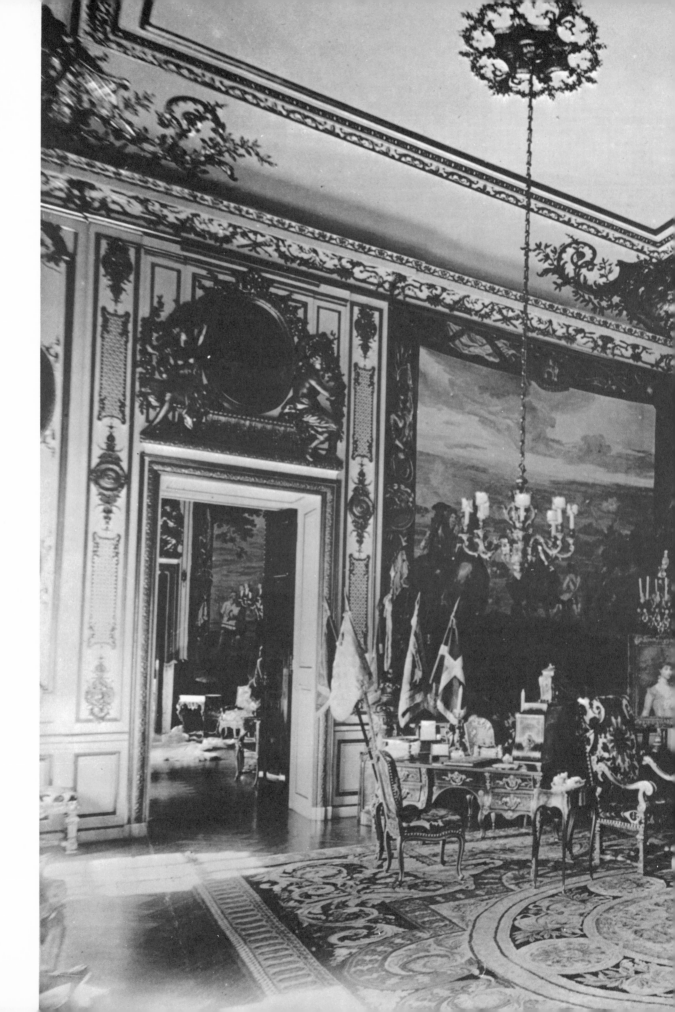

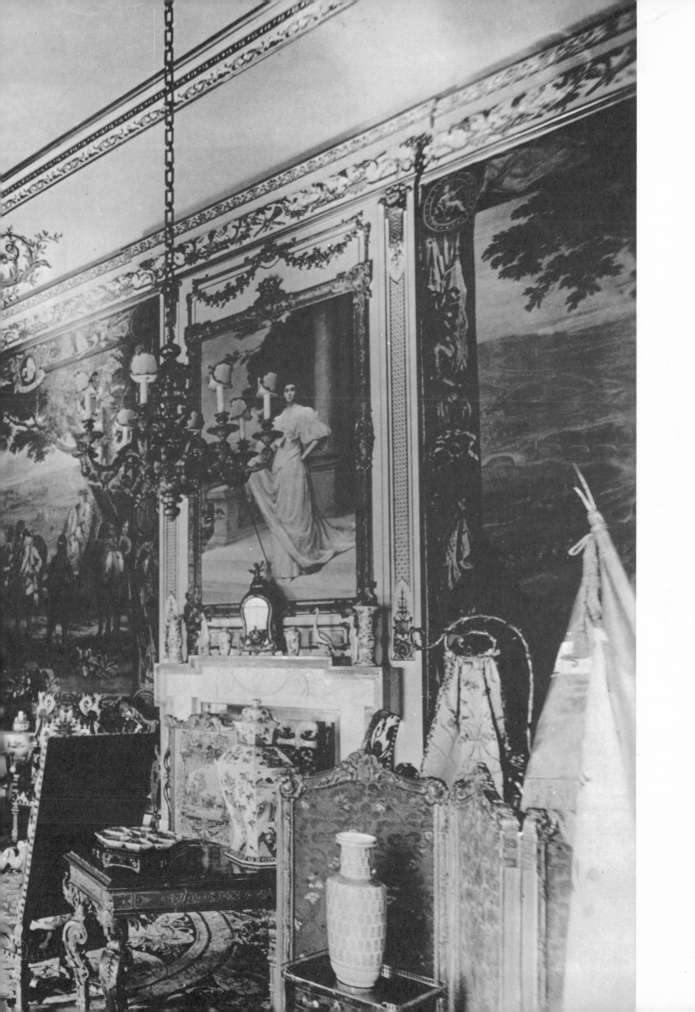

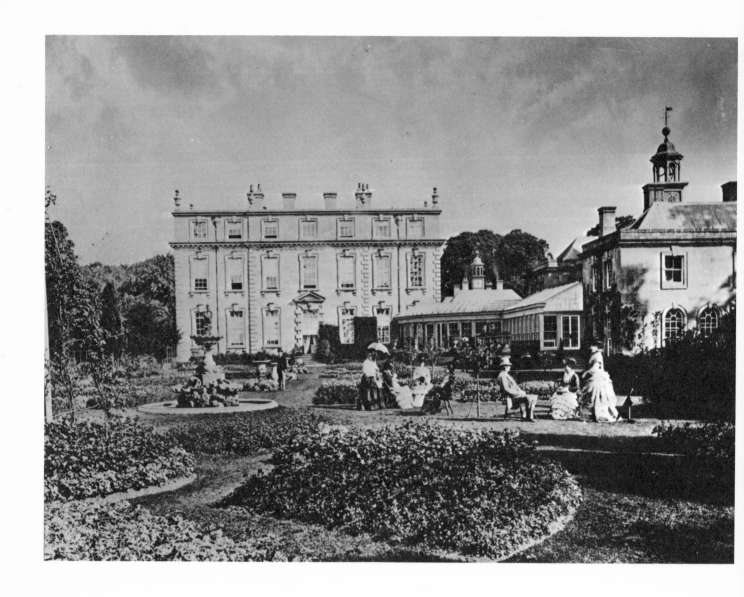

89 *previous page* The first State Room at Blenheim
Palace, Woodstock, designed by Vanbrugh. The interior
shows de Hondt's tapestries portraying the first Duke of
Marlborough's victories; and Duvain's portrait of
Consuelo who was married to the ninth Duke.

90 A formal gathering in the garden at Ditchley Park,
Oxfordshire, *c.* 1870, then the seat of Viscount Dillon.
It is the third great eighteenth-century mansion of
Oxfordshire after Blenheim and Heythrop House. A fine
example of the Palladian school of architecture, it was
designed by James Gibbs and built in 1722.

91 The parish church of St Lawrence's at North
Hinksey, near Oxford, which dates back to Norman times.
The photograph, showing Taunt in the foreground, was
probably taken by his assistant *c.* 1870.

92 A group of children at Downs Bottom Cottages,
West Ilsley in the Berkshire Downs in 1897. It was here
at his mother's home that Taunt spent the summer
holidays of his childhood.

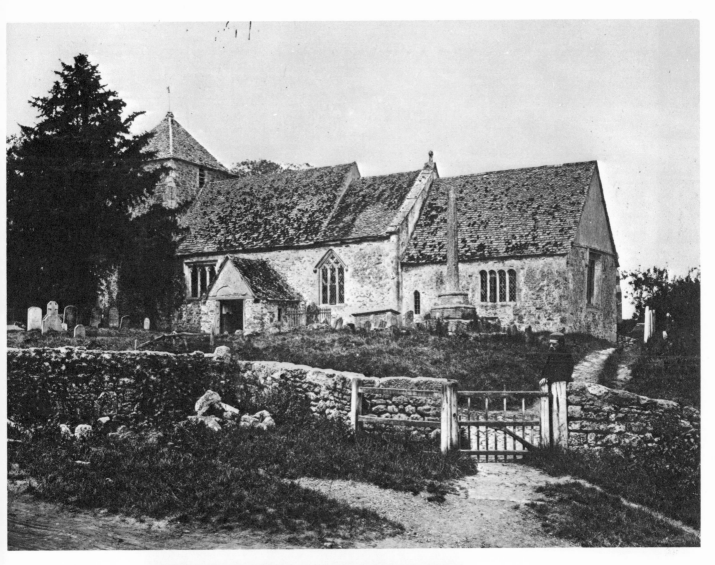

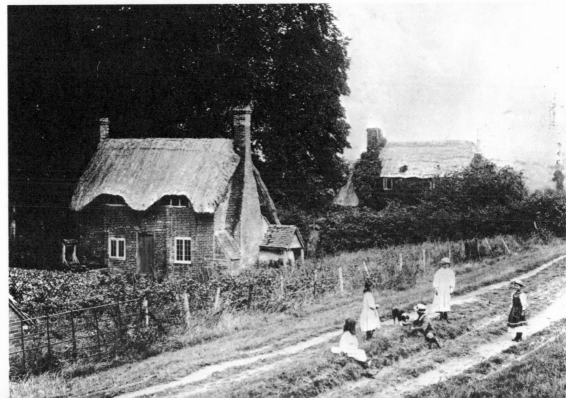

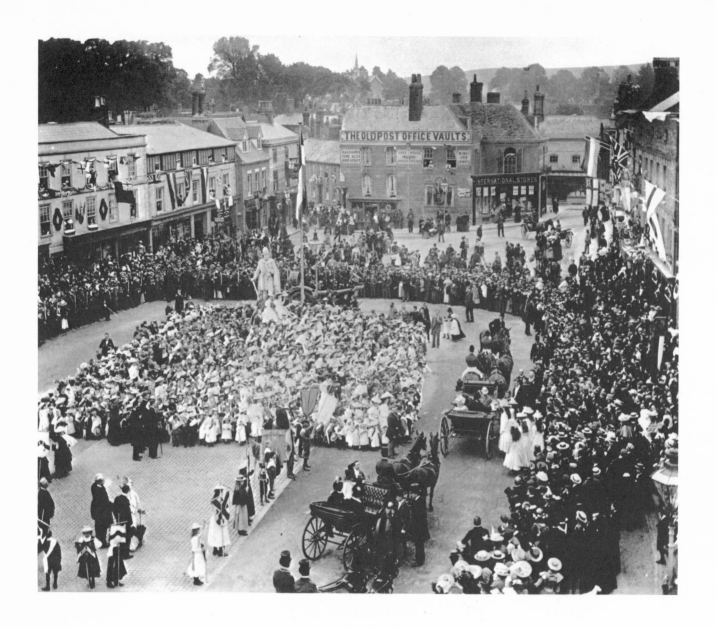

93   The visit of the Prince and Princess of Wales, later King Edward VII and Queen Alexandra, to Wantage to stay with Lord Wantage at Lockinge on 13 June 1898. The children grouped on a raised platform around the statue of King Alfred in the market place sang the National Anthem when the couple arrived. The young ladies of the town are presenting bouquets.

94   Witney Fair, September 1904, with a steam roundabout, a prominent feature at country fairs. The blanket-makers released from their toil enjoyed themselves with great enthusiasm.

95   The weaving shed in one of the blanket factories at Witney, containing a hundred looms. A blanket took an hour to weave, but it was not cut at this stage. Weaving continued until all the warp was used when some fourteen to twenty-eight blankets were completed. The girls were paid by the weight of weft used.

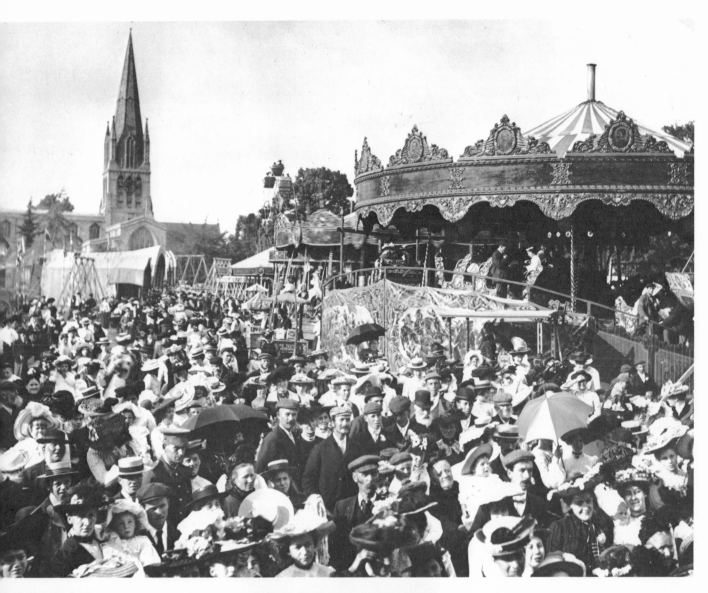

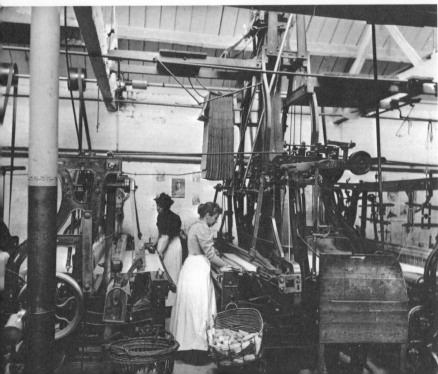

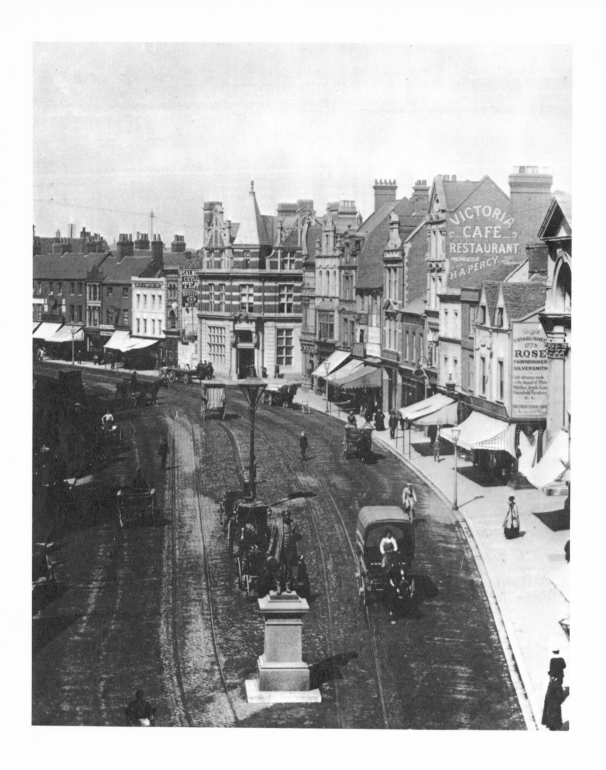

96   Broad Street, Reading, with the bronze statue of
George Palmer – of the famous Huntley and Palmer
biscuit company – taken shortly after its unveiling in
1891. It has now been removed to Palmer Park.

97   Looking up the Kingsbury at Aylesbury,
Buckinghamshire, at the Jubilee celebrations in 1887.

98   Hart Street, Henley-on-Thames, c. 1885. The
drinking fountain has now been removed.

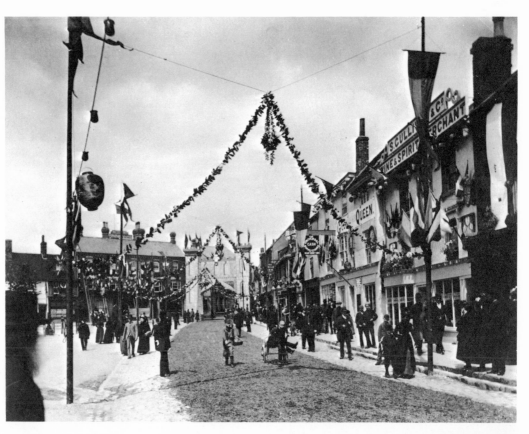

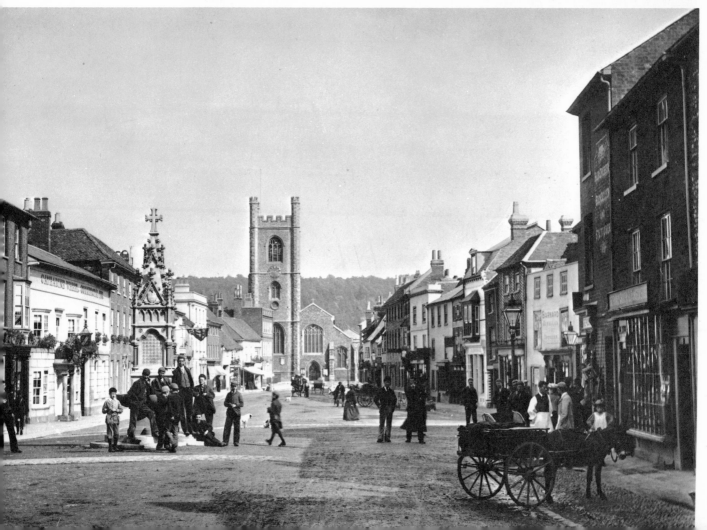

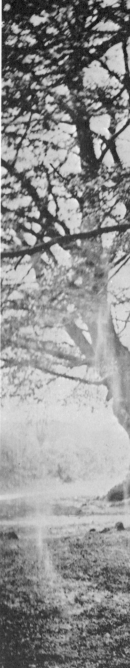

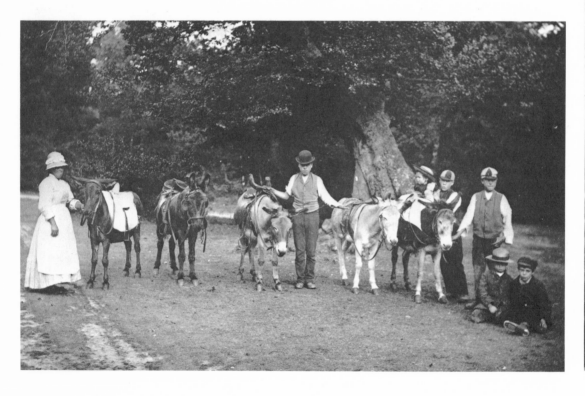

99   Burnham Beeches in Buckinghamshire. The donkeys must have formed a favourite attraction for children at bank holidays and for weekend picnic outings, *c*. 1880.

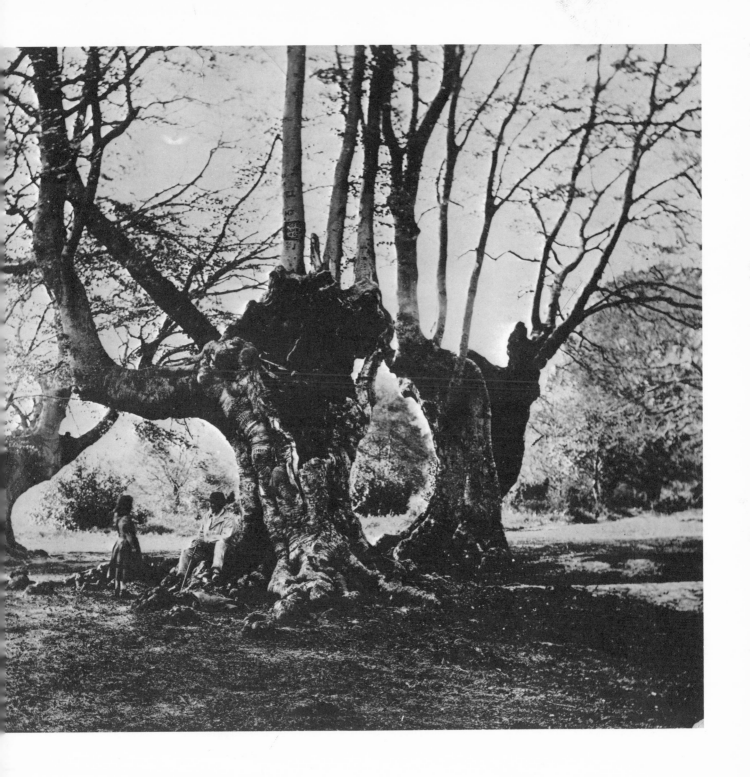

100 This earlier picture of Burnham Beeches, *c.* 1870, has a strange ethereal quality. The light filtering through the branches seems almost magical.

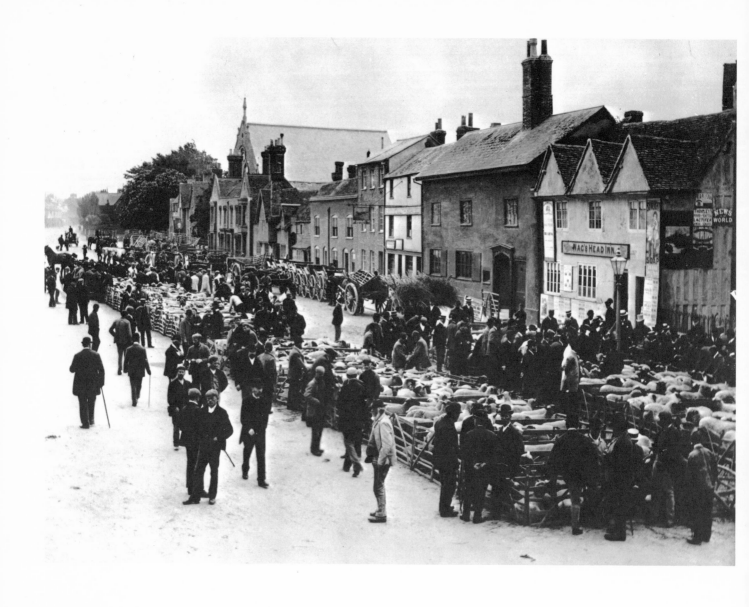

101 Two street-market scenes when the whole town was taken over for the sale, in days when the livelihood of most country people depended on agriculture and livestock. This first photograph shows the sheepmarket in Cornmarket, Thame, Oxfordshire, 1897.

102 A horse fair at Bampton, Oxfordshire in 1904.

103 A canal or narrow boat at Wantage Wharf, below the church, on the Wilts & Berks canal in May 1895.

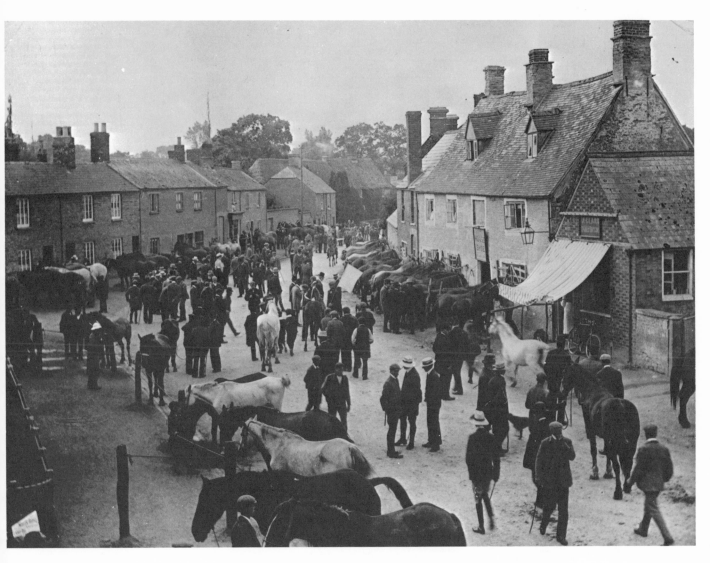

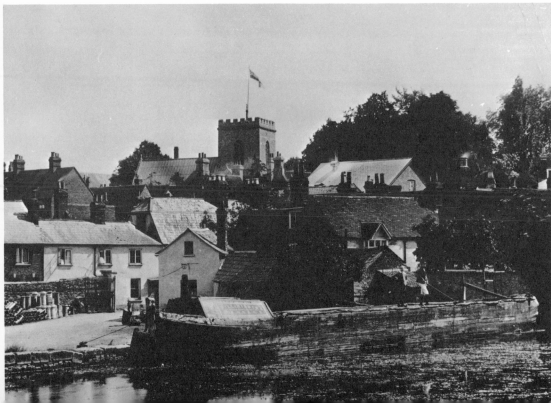

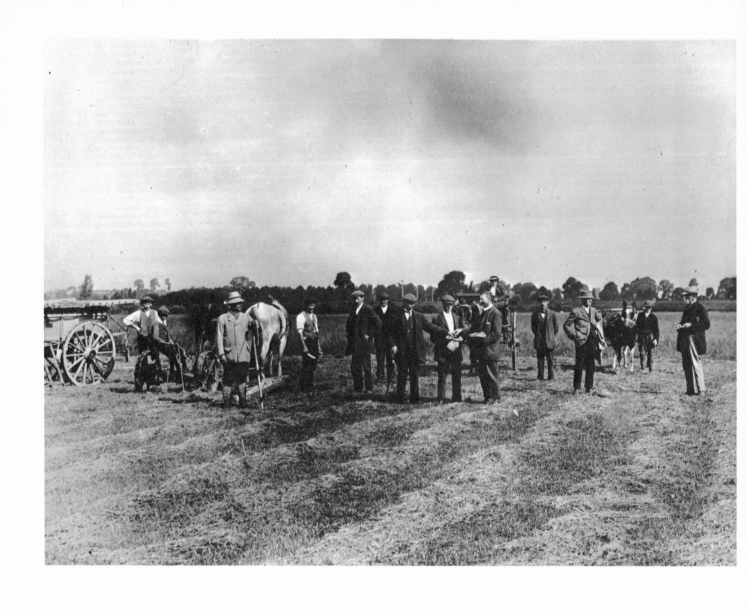

104   Drawing lots for meadowland at West Mead, Yarnton, Oxford in 1918. This occasion is a rare survival of the open field agricultural system, and takes place when the owners of the eighty acres of parish land each draw from a bag one of the thirteen holly wood balls at hay time, to ensure a fair share of grass for mowing and grazing rights.

Taunt's Travels

This selection of photographs is taken from Taunt's work outside Oxford and his home counties. His travelling was mostly confined to the south of England and includes Gloucestershire, Warwickshire, Leicestershire, Hampshire and Cornwall. Unlike Francis Frith and Samuel Bourne, Henry Taunt was not of a globe-trotting nature. Most of his photographs derive from an intimate and personal look at the familiar English countryside.

He had a long and close relationship with the Cotswolds and he portrays the mellow stone and homely towns and villages with the love of a native. His pictures of London show us a very different capital in an age when one had time and space in which to appreciate its architecture. The Avon of Shakespeare was Taunt's second river and he shows its mills and waterside cottages in the lovely Warwickshire countryside. The graceful masted boats at Southampton and Falmouth contrast sharply with the iron ships that were to follow.

His travelling activities also encompassed the well-known national monuments. He photographed them either as commissions or for the production of some publication or series of postcards he was engaged upon. Taunt's photographs of many such outstanding items form an important part of the collection at the National Monuments Record.

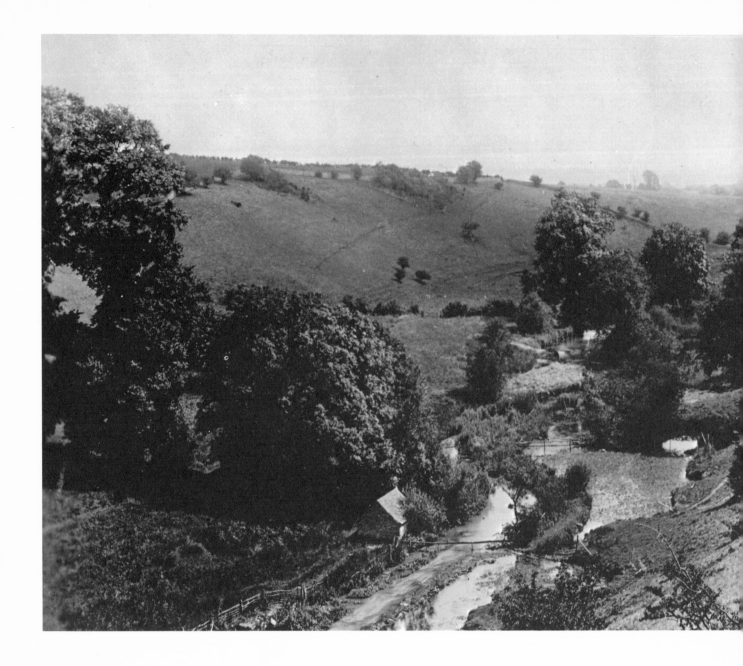

The Cotswolds

105 The Windrush valley, Gloucestershire, *c.* 1885. This lovely tributary which joins the Thames at Newbridge flows through the heart of the Cotswold country.

106 The procession down the High Street at Chipping Campden Hiring Fair or 'Mop' in 1896.

One of the old institutions which still remain in the Cotswolds is the annual 'mop' or hiring fair.

. . . Every labouring man in the district hurries into the town, where all sorts of entertainments are held in the market-place, including 'whirly-go-rounds', discordant music and the usual 'shows' which go to make up a country fair. 'Hiring' used to be the great feature of these fairs. In the days before local newspapers were invented every sort of servant, from a farm bailiff to a maid-of-all-work, was hired for the year at the annual mop. The word 'mop' is derived from an old custom which ordained that the maid-servants who came to find situations should bring their badge of office with them to the fair. They came with their brooms and mops, just as a carter would tie a piece of whipcord to his coat, and a shepherd's hat would be decorated with a tuft of wool.

J. Arthur Gibbs, *A Cotswold Village*, 1899

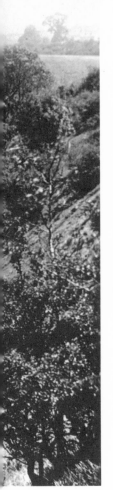

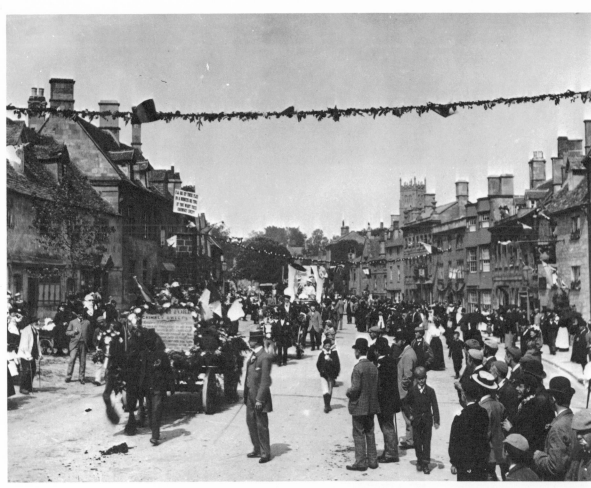

107   Children at the lower well near
Stow-on-the-Wold, Gloucestershire,
c. 1885. The boy standing had obviously
not graduated to a position in life where
he could wear trousers. He is still wearing
a dress probably handed down from an
elder sister.

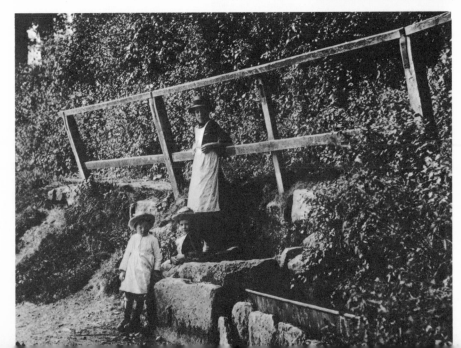

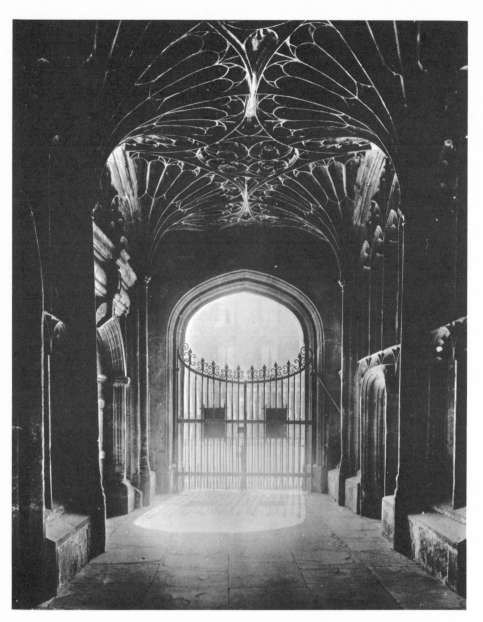
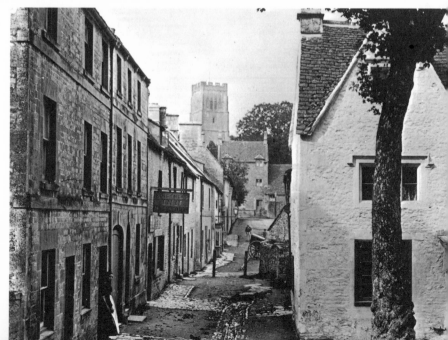

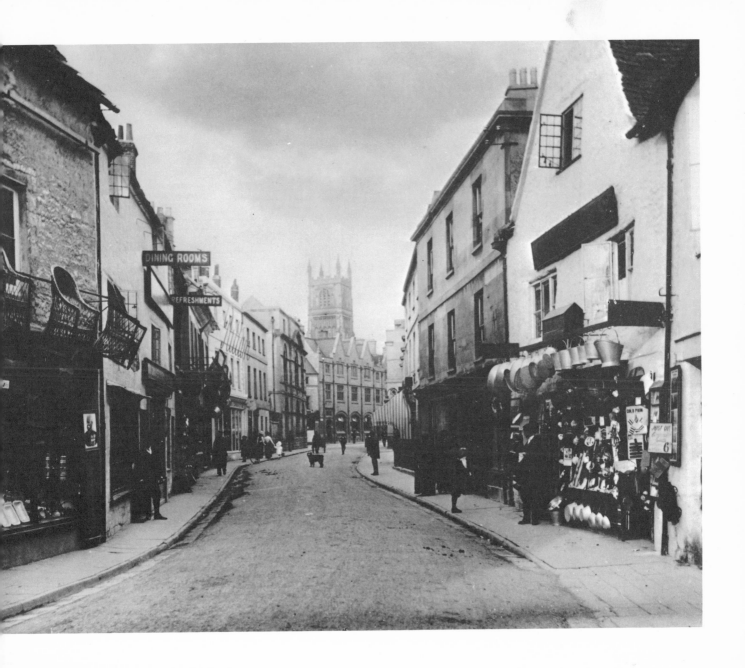

108   Delicate fan-tracery groining in the fifteenth-century porch of St John-the-Baptist Church, Cirencester. One of the finest parish churches in England, it dates back to the great days of the Cotswold wool industry.

109   Cotswold stone houses at Northleach, Gloucestershire, 1901.

110   The wares of country-town shops on display in Castle Street, Cirencester – the capital of the Cotswolds, 1901. Cirencester still remains a beautiful and unspoiled country market-town.

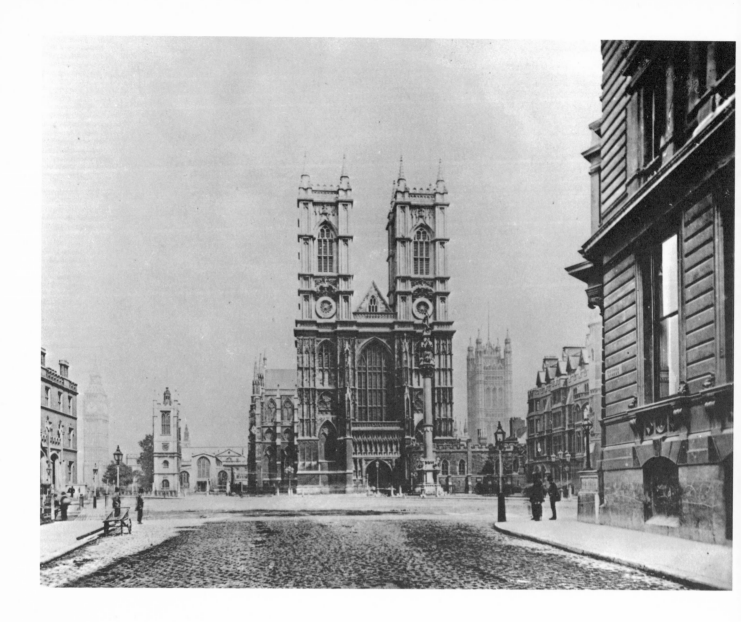

London

111   A general view of Westminster Abbey taken from the west, *c. 1870*.

112   Trafalgar Square, without people or pigeons!

113   Cleopatra's Needle and Westminster Embankment from Charing Cross, looking towards the old Waterloo Bridge and Somerset House, *c. 1880*. The photograph was taken shortly after Sir Erasmus Wilson brought the monument to England.

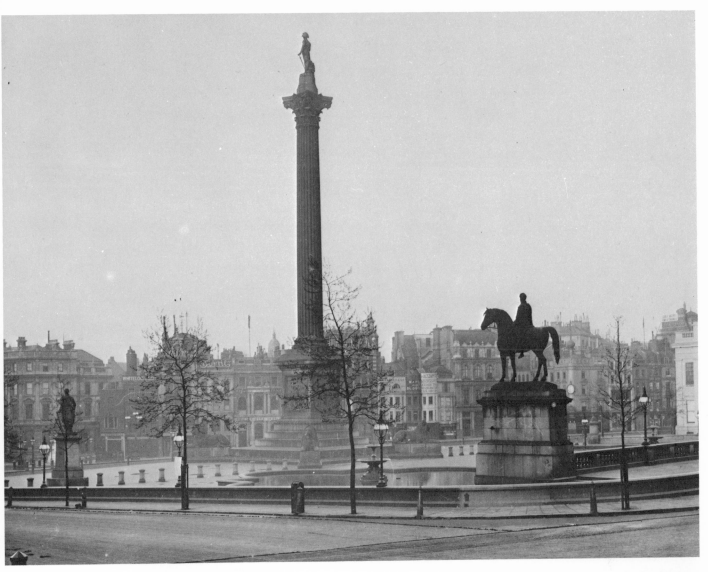

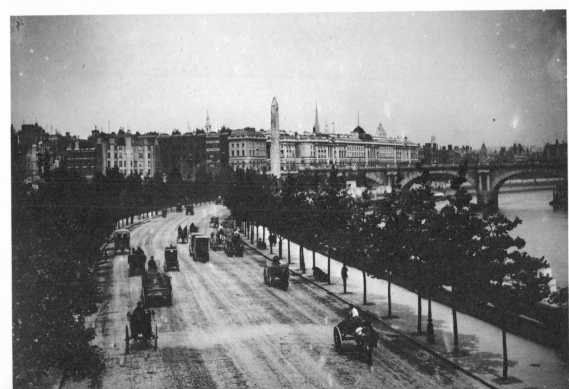

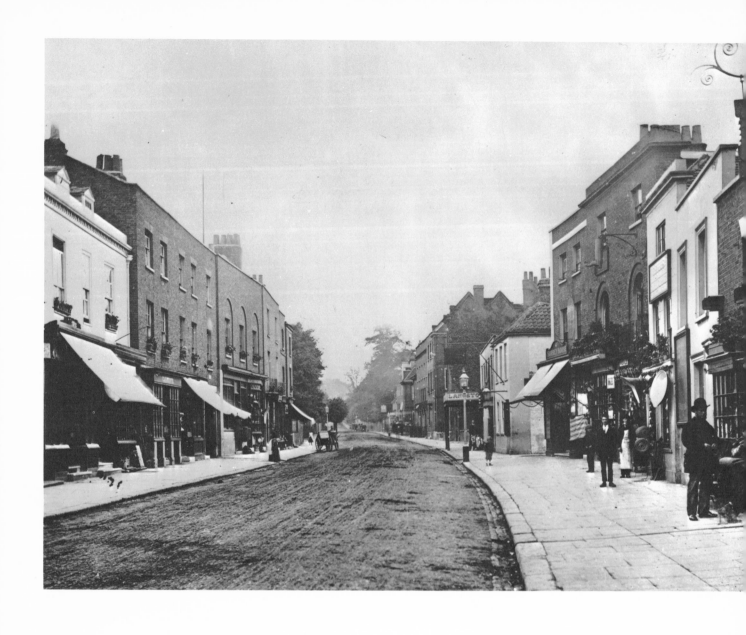

114   Putney High Street, *c.* 1870. Few commuters today
could ever find this street so deserted.

Cornwall

115   The Fish Market at Falmouth, *c.* 1875.

116 *following page*   The quay and fishing boats at
Falmouth, *c.* 1875.

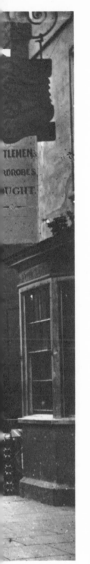
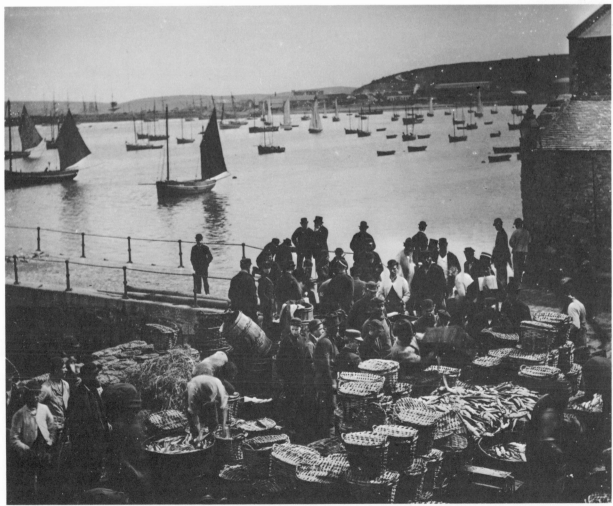

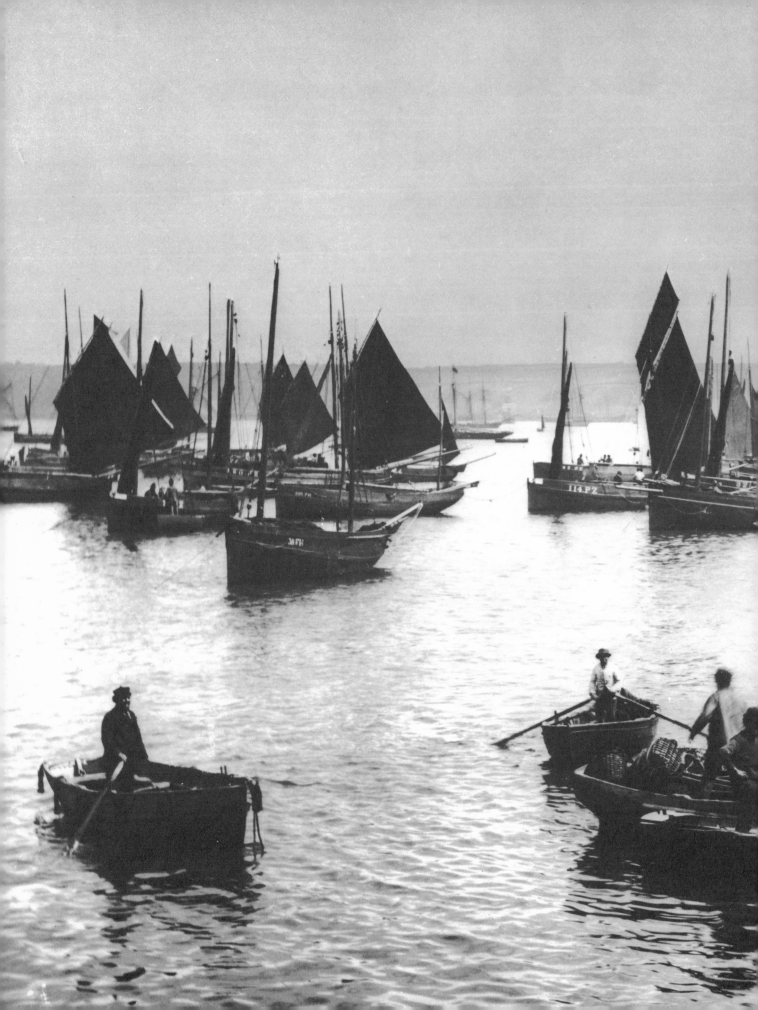

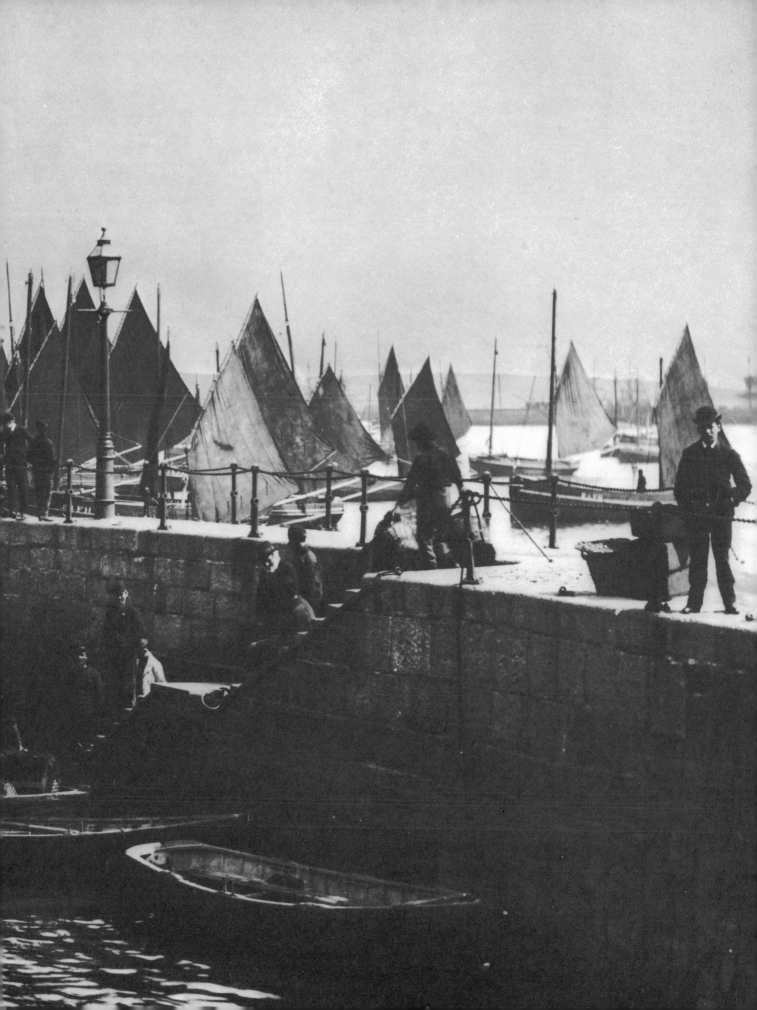

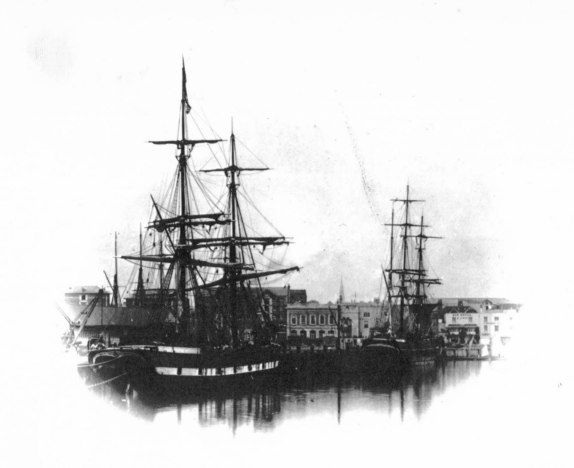

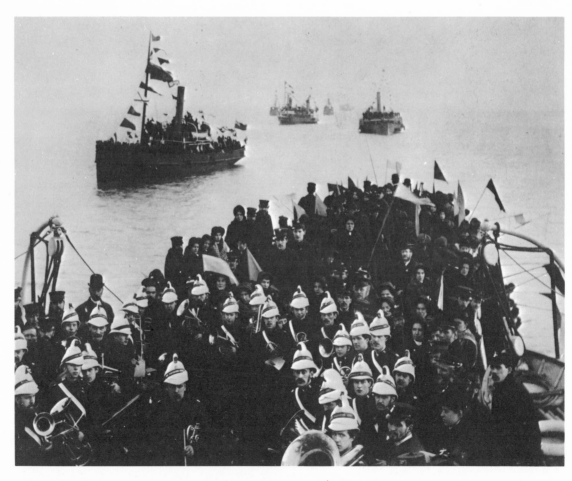

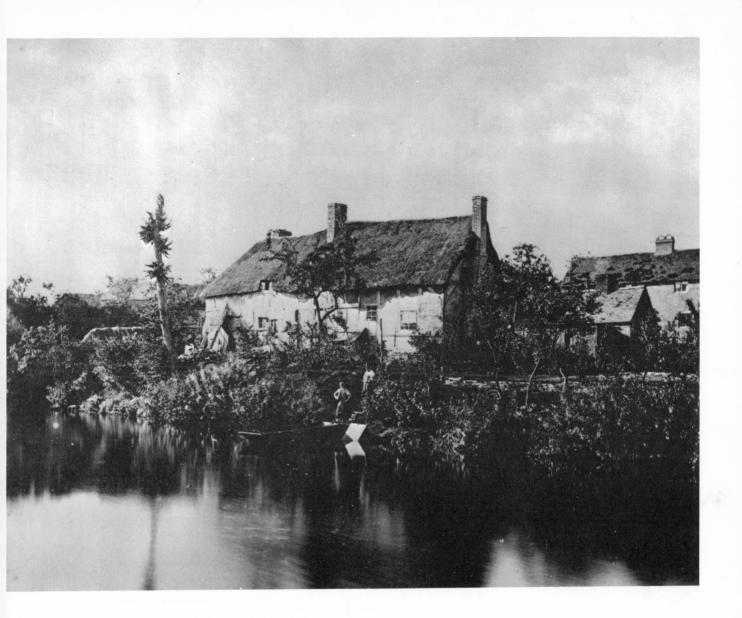

Hampshire

117   The jetty at Southampton with two-masted vessels, *c.* 1880.

118   Southampton, on board the *Prince of Wales*, with a Salvation Army band in 1892.

Stratford. the Avon and Warwickshire

119   Old cottages, one probably the dwelling of a fisherman, at Alveston, Warwickshire, from the River Avon, *c.* 1875.

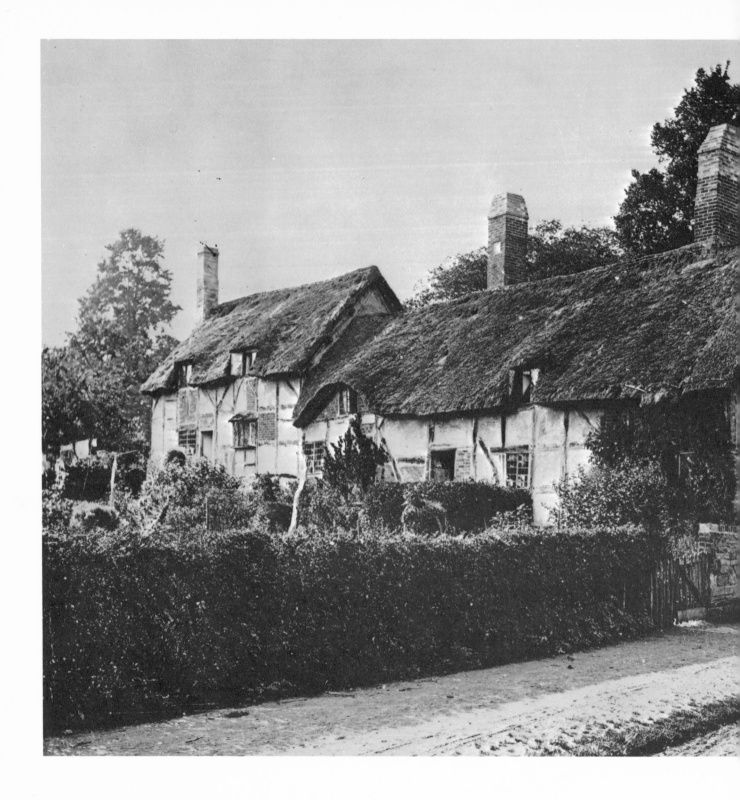

120 A popular tourist attraction, Anne Hathaway's cottage at Shottery near Stratford, in 1875.

121 The original Shakespeare Memorial Theatre at Stratford-upon-Avon, situated on the west bank, photographed when the building was nearly complete in 1878. It was burnt down in 1926.

122 Nafford Mill, now disappeared, was situated between Pershore and Tewkesbury on the Avon. The river here was at its most picturesque, c. 1870.

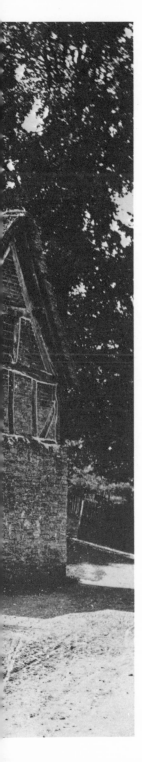

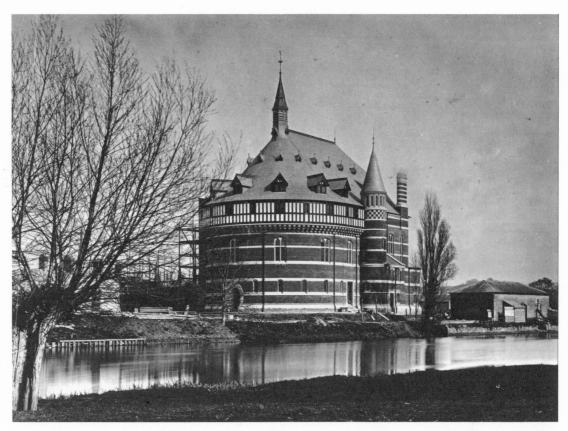

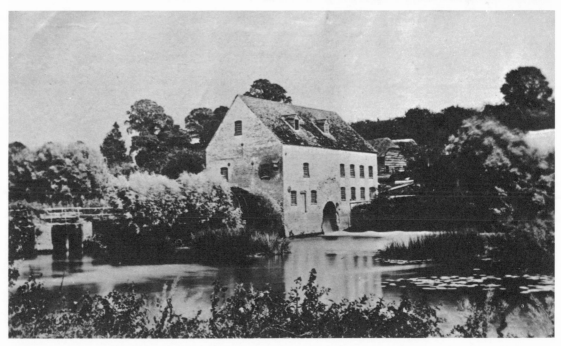

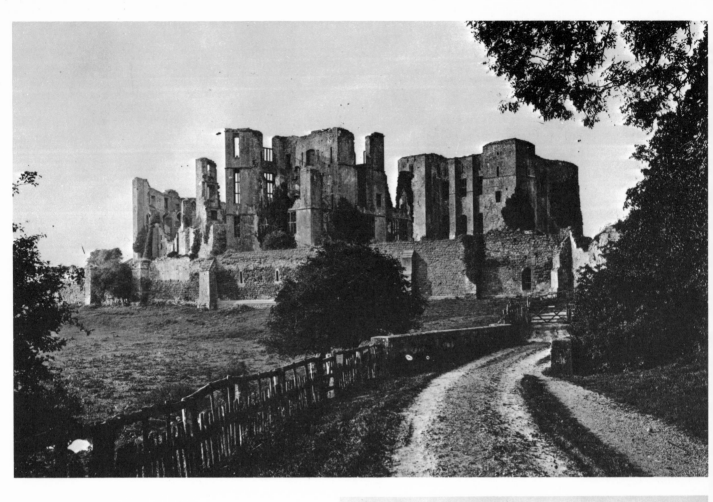

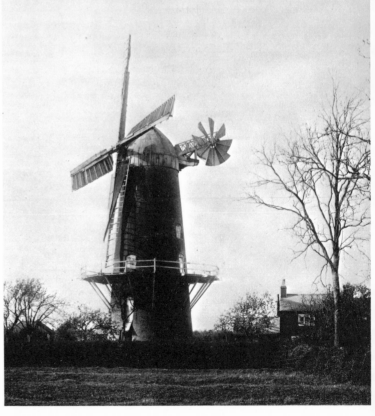

123   Kenilworth Castle, Warwickshire, *c.* 1870.

Leicestershire

124   The brick-tower windmill at Lutterworth,
Leicestershire, *c.* 1880. It was situated on the east side of
Leicester Road and apparently was paid for by
subscription and built about 1800. It was demolished in
the early years of this century.

Portraits

Faces seemed to hold an intense fascination for Henry Taunt. Many of his portraits were commissioned, others he took for his own enjoyment; but all are photographs of character. The subjects almost breathe: look into the eyes of the Berkshire shepherd (Plate 130), or at the arrogance of the old Oxford man (Plate 132), or the day-dreaming wistfulness of the lady at Dorchester Abbey (Plate 131). These are not careful studio pieces like the portraits of Julia Margaret Cameron and Nadar, but shrewd observations of people in their own environment.

Taunt's portraits range right across society, from future King or Prime Minister to the oldest village inhabitants and playful children. But each is in perfect sympathy with the subject. Disraeli seems to have the worries of the world on his shoulders; or is he perhaps more than a little bored with his company? The future King appears aggressive and proud. The villagers look pensively toward their future, perhaps an almshouse in which to end their days.

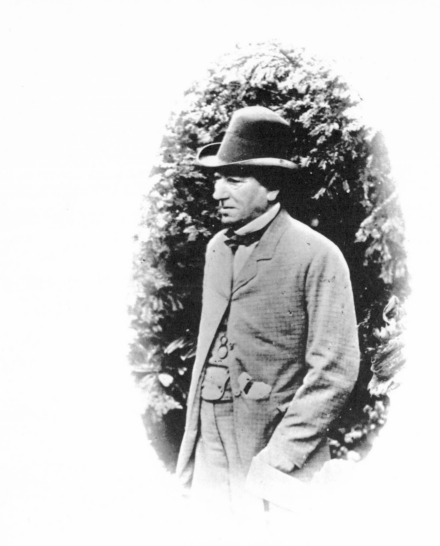

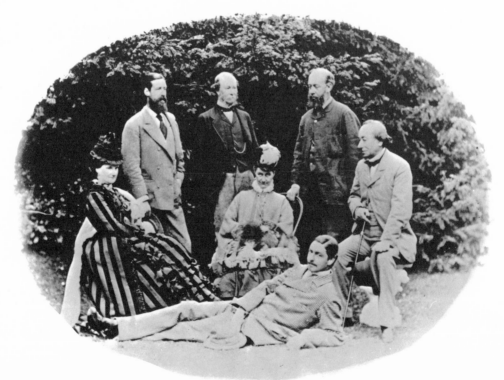

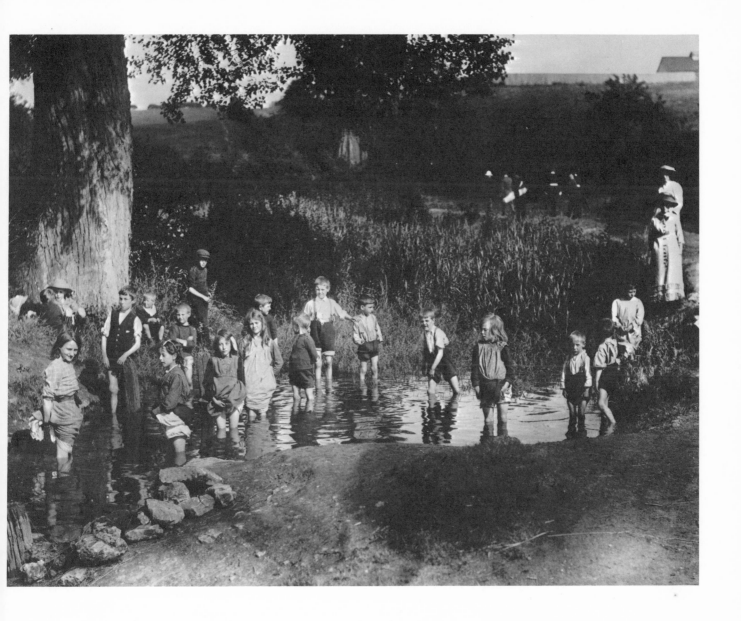

125   Benjamin Disraeli, later to become Earl of
Beaconsfield, taken at his country home, Hughendon, in
1874. This was the first year of his second, and most
successful, period as Prime Minister.

126   A group taken at Hughendon on the same occasion:
(standing left to right) Lord Rowton, Lord Bradford,
Lord Wharncliffe; (seated left to right) Lady Bradford,
Lady Wharncliffe, Benjamin Disraeli; (in the foreground)
Lord Pembroke.

127   Cowley children playing 'ducks and drakes', in a
sheep washing-place at the Cowley Marsh in July 1914.

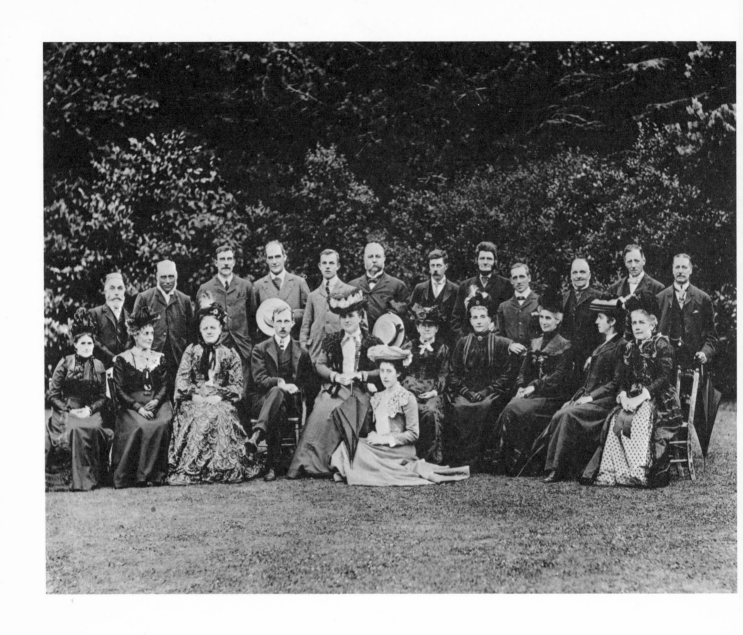

Two groups of a very different social order, taken at about the same date.

128   The Morrell family of Headington Hill Hall, Oxford, owners of the well-known Oxford brewery. The photograph is taken on the occasion of the coming-of-age of Mr J. H. Morrell (seated fourth from left) on 9 July 1903. The group includes, besides members of the family, the brewery manager, bailiff, coachman, waterman, housekeeper, butler, gardener, schoolteacher and nurse.

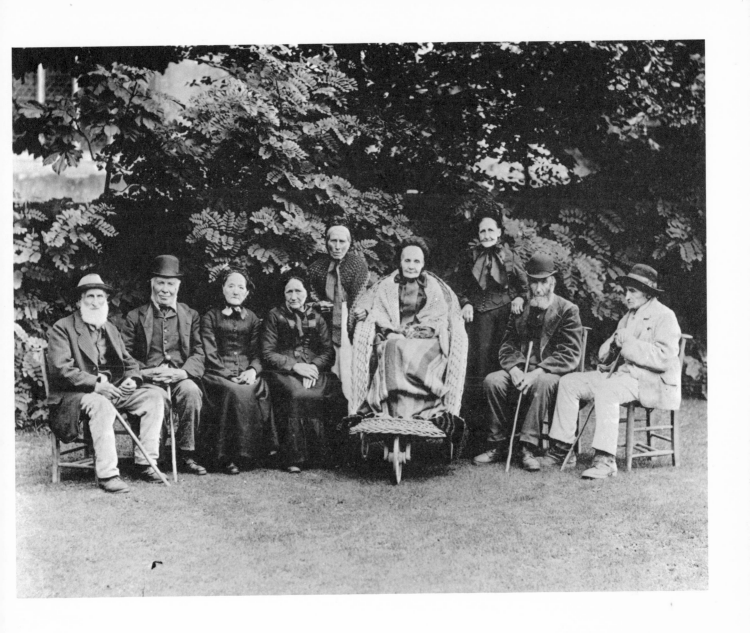

129   The oldest inhabitants of the village, West Ilsley, Berkshire, *c.* 1900.

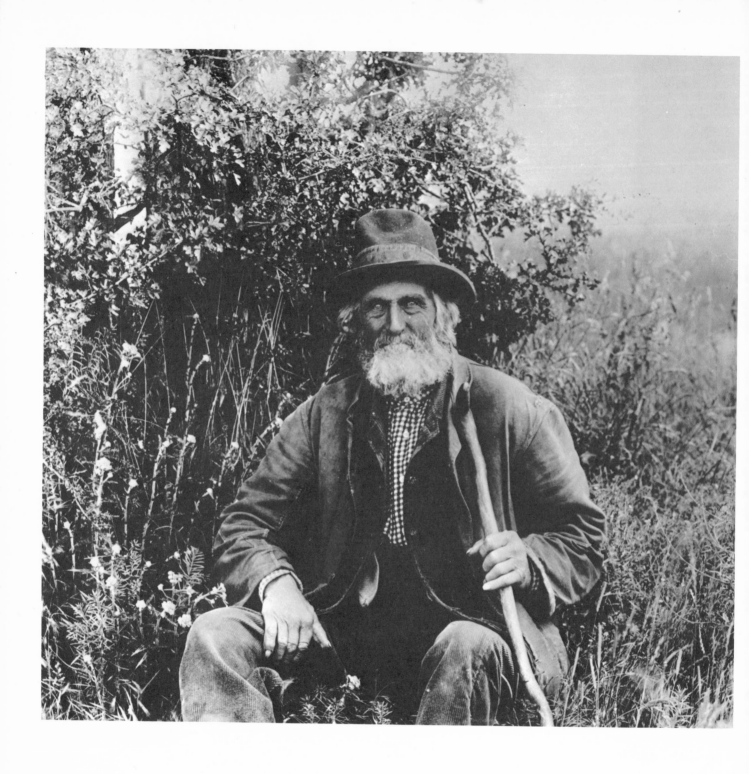

130   A Berkshire shepherd, *c.* 1890.

131   An old lady at Dorchester Abbey, Dorchester-on-Thames, *c.* 1905.

132   Harris, an Oxford inhabitant, 1907.

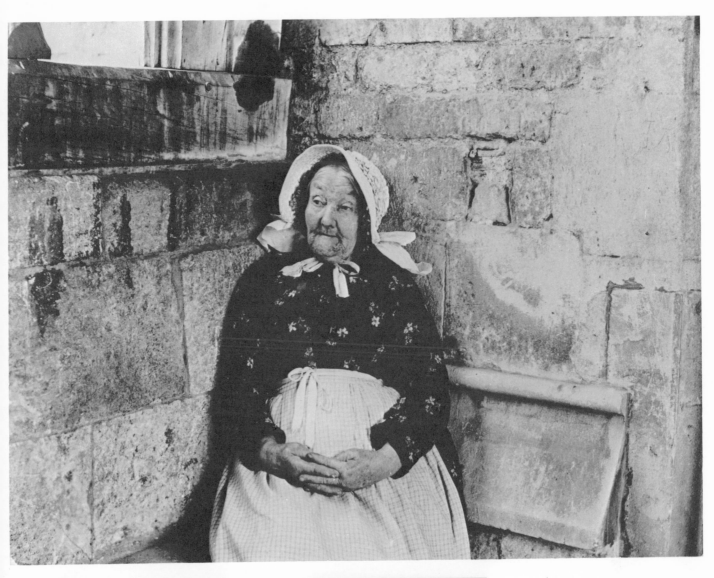

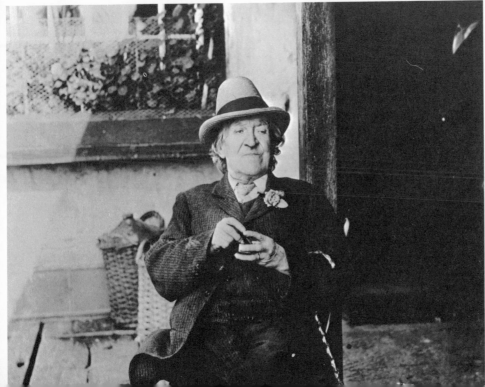

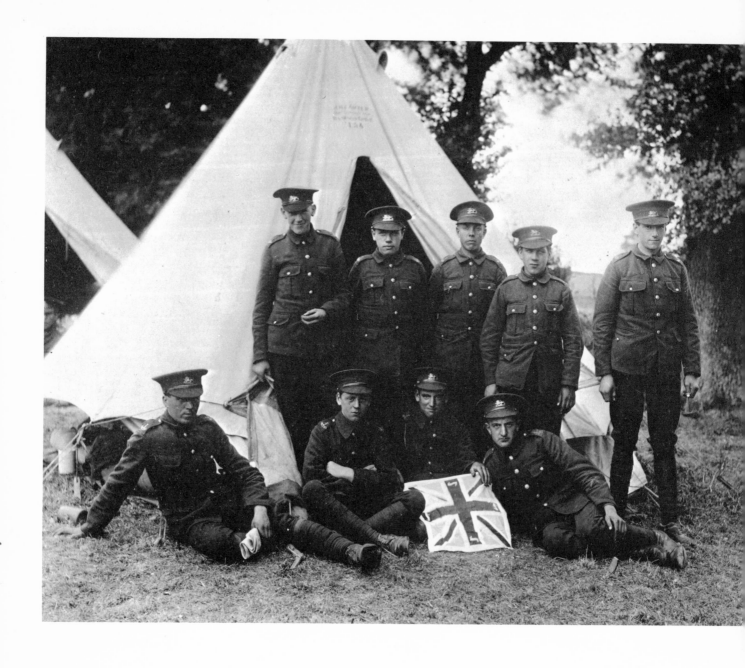

133 Their fate awaiting: Tent 154, Didcot Camp, Berkshire, 1914.

134 The Prince of Wales, later Edward VII, as Colonel-in-Chief of the Queen's Own Oxfordshire Hussars.

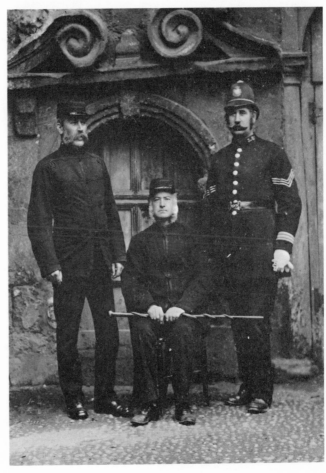

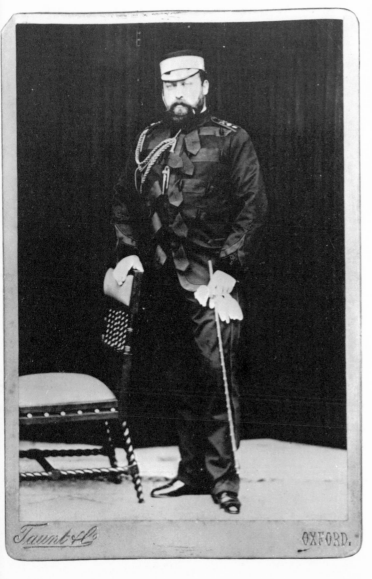

135 Oxford policemen in the doorway of Nixons School
in the Old Town Hall Yard, *c.* 1890. Inspector Dixon,
Chief Constable Head and Sergeant Miller.

136 *following page*   Mr A. Harcourt with the Nuneham
Cricket XI in 1888. It seems the gentlemen are in whites and
sporting caps whilst the village lads are dressed in less
formal attire.

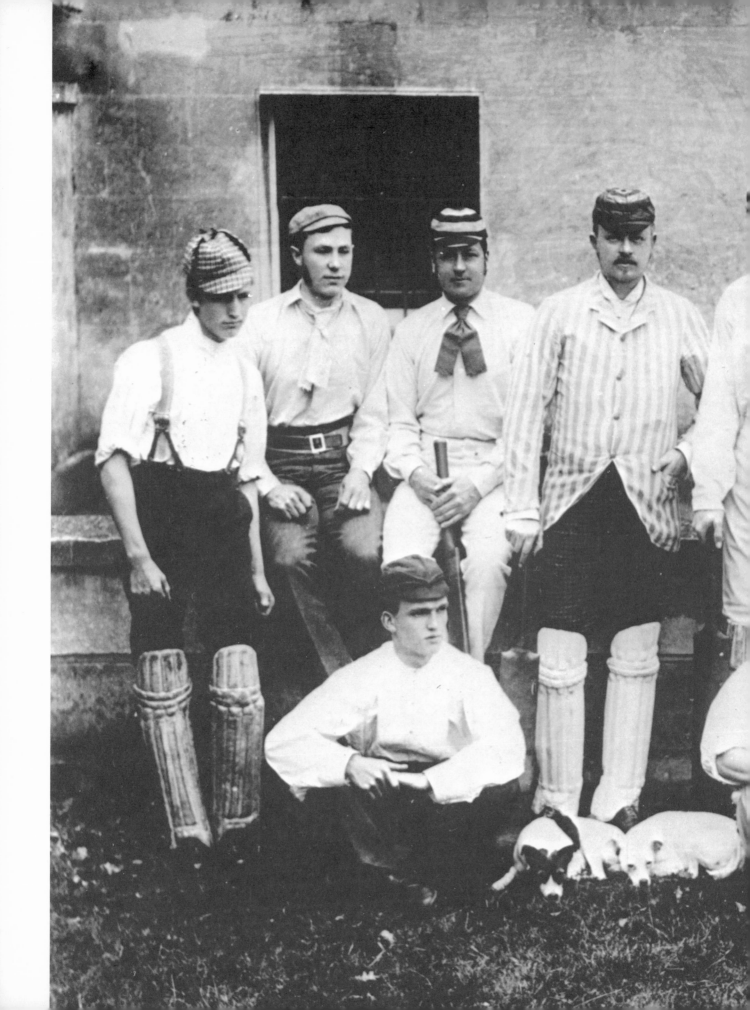

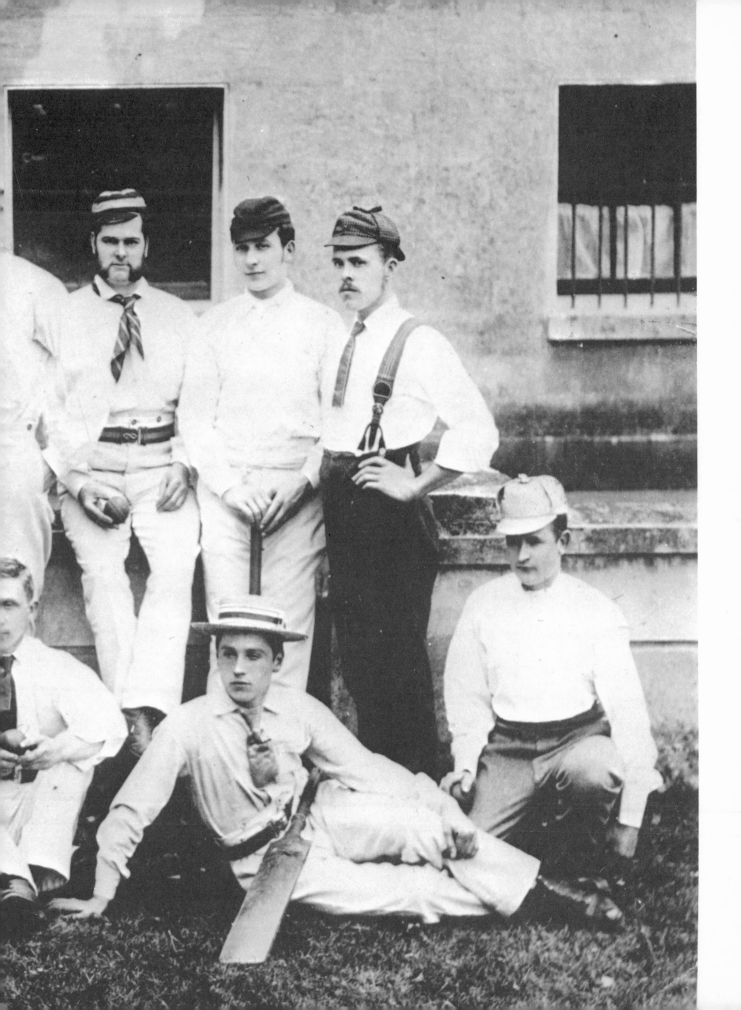

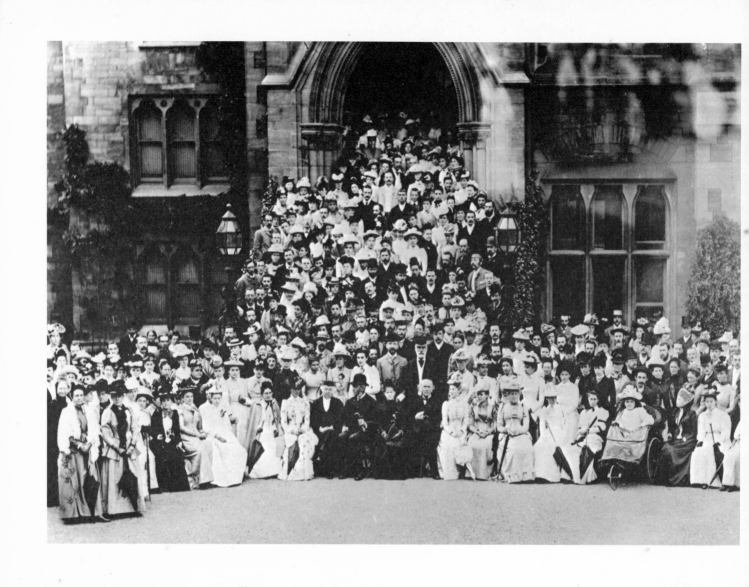

137 An early Oxford University Summer Extension School, taken on the steps of Balliol Hall in 1887. Benjamin Jowett, Master of Balliol, and Sir Henry Acland, Regius Professor of Medicine, are seated next to the ladies. This is probably the first photograph ever taken of Jowett, who was always a reluctant sitter.

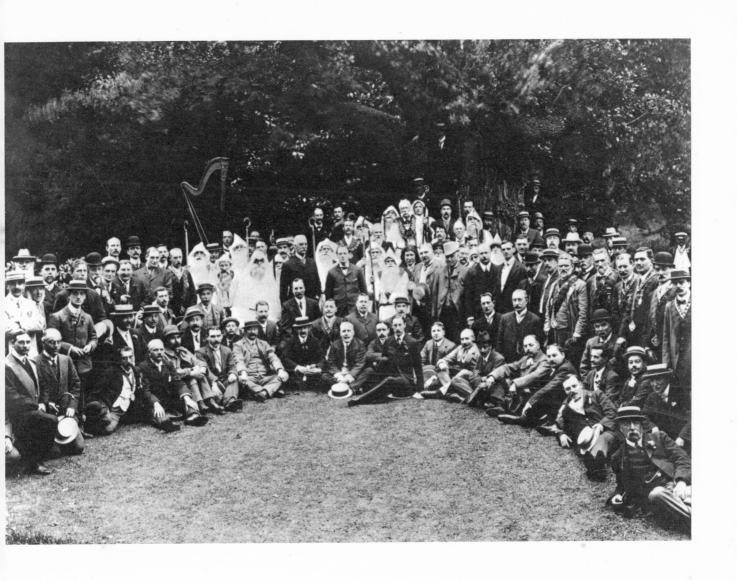

138 A red-letter-day in Oxford Druidism: the initiation of Winston Spencer Churchill M.P., soon to become First Lord of the Admiralty. The ceremony took place on 11 August 1908 in the grounds of Blenheim Palace, and the ninth Duke of Marlborough is seated prominently in the foreground.

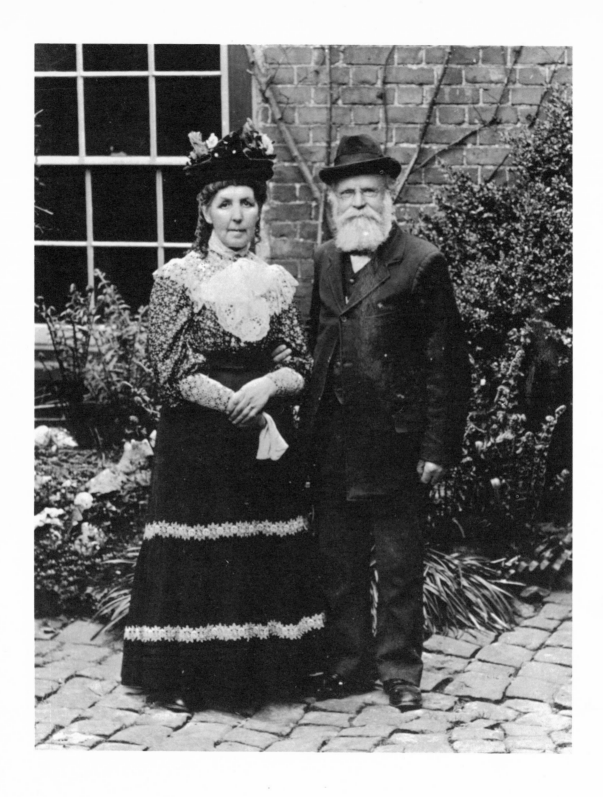

139 Mr and Mrs Samuel Adcock, of Princes Risborough, Bucks, in April 1908.
They sold Taunt's postcards and guides in the 'Risboro' post office which formed
part of their grocery and stationery shop. Adcock lived in 'Risboro' for seventy-six
years.

Victorian and Edwardian Life

'A Hotch Potch, a medley of things instructive and amusing' is perhaps how Henry Taunt would have introduced this section. It is a group of photographs that individually could have come under other headings but as a selection they capitalize on the idiosyncrasies of the period. Henry Taunt was by nature a traditionalist and he was aware that the encroachment of nineteenth-century industrialization was rapidly changing the scenes he could remember of his boyhood days in the 1850s. I believe that it was in his mind that the established lifestyle with its strict social order was destined for change and perceptively he recorded it with his camera. He shows us the customs associated with the seasons of the year, street entertainers and processions, various means of transport and people at their work.

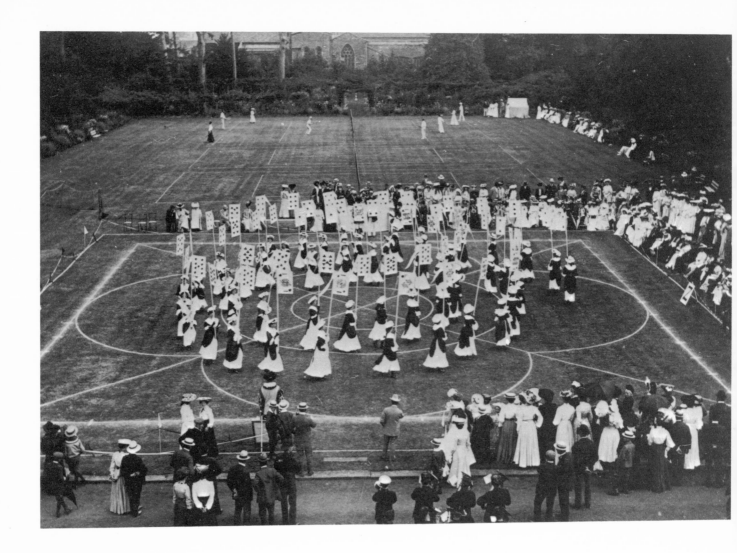

140   The country gentry amuse themselves at a game of living bridge played on the lawns of Faringdon House, at the Faringdon Flower Show, Berkshire, July 1906.

141   The village children in a May Day procession at Iffley near Oxford in 1906. The traditions at Iffley were well established, with their own songs preserved at the school. The girls wore white starched dresses with blue or pink sashes and wreathes of flowers on their heads. The boys carried coloured wooden staves dressed with flowers and ribbons. The whole court consisted of about forty children including the King and Queen, maids of honour, treasurers, garlanders, guards, mace-bearers and two bigger boys as policemen to keep order. The May Queen during this particular year was my wife's great aunt, Phyllis Ludlow.

142   The Bidford Men, Morris Dancers at Chipping Campden, c. 1890. This was a well-known group with Clown and Hobby Horse and are still noted for their last dance called 'Morrice off' which continued as long as the leader had breath. The dancers come from Shakespeare's 'Drunken Bidford', a village between Stratford and Evesham.

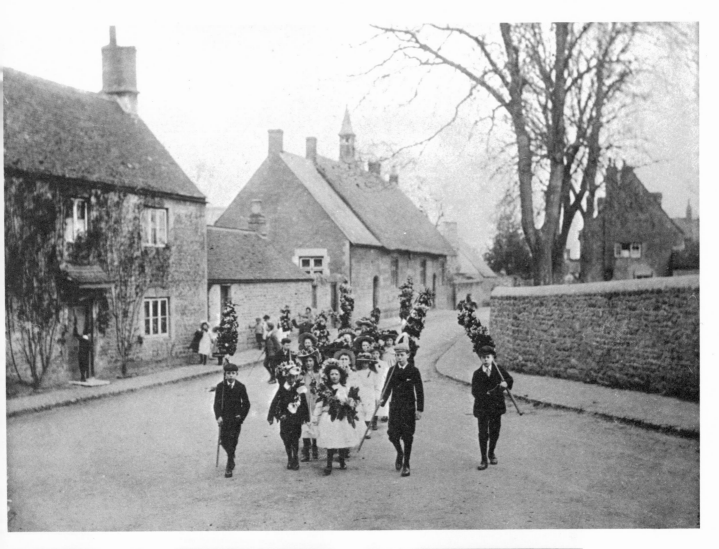

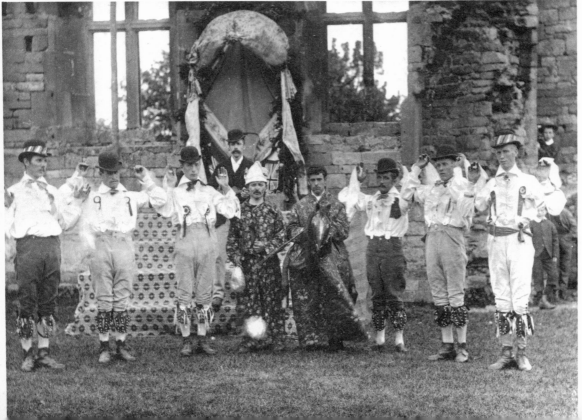

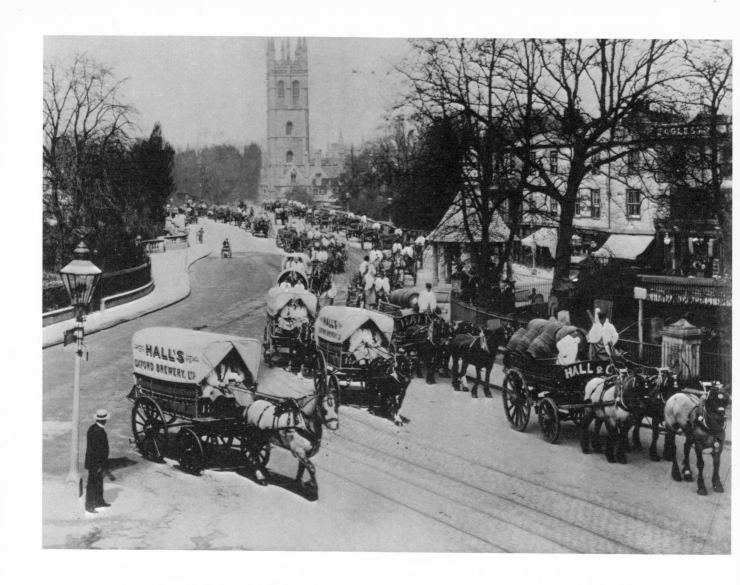

143 A May Day procession of drays belonging to Hall's Oxford brewery company, which has now been taken over. Magdalen Bridge in the background looks wider than it should and I think has been the subject of Taunt's artistic licence.

144 The Druids' float in an Oddfellows' procession on Magdalen Bridge on Whit Monday 1898. The Noble Arch and Bards in full dress are seated beneath an oak tree.

145 A group of Oxford University Rifle Volunteers at their annual camp on Headington Hill in the 1880s. The grounds were at the home of their colonel, G. H. Morrell M.P.

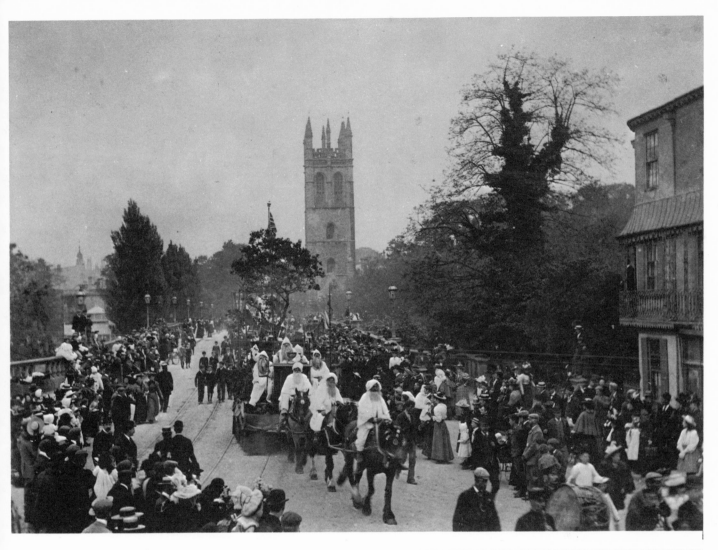

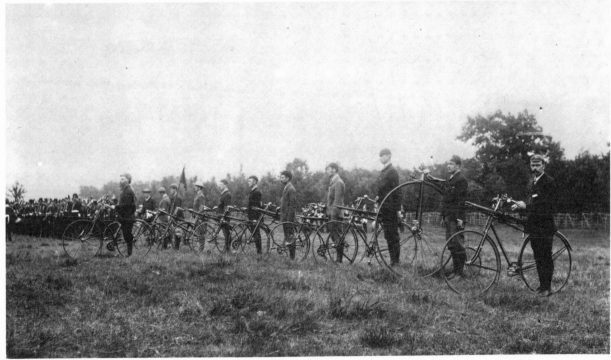

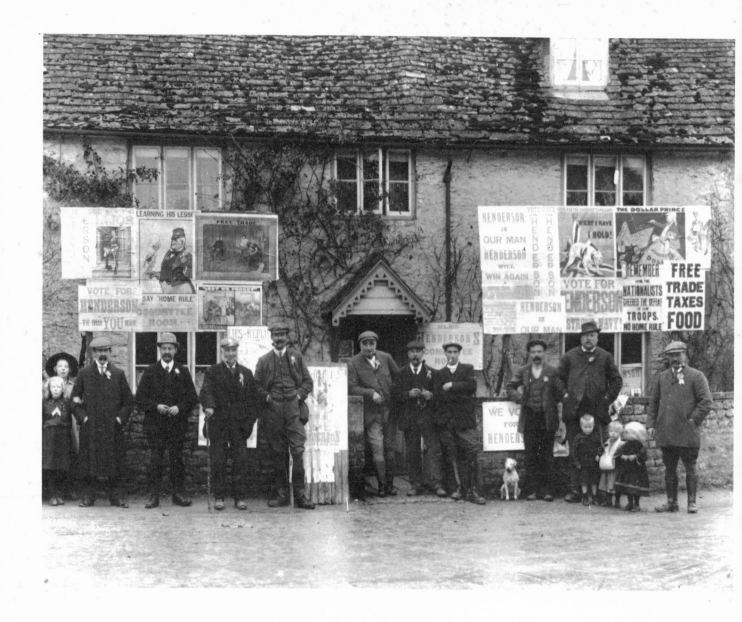

146 A typical group of farmers outside a Conservative Committee Room in North Berkshire, December 1910. The Conservative candidate, Major Henderson, was returned for a second time in that year of two general elections.

147 A one-man band, on the right of the photograph, with musical companion and monkey at a Buckinghamshire village, c. 1900. To the village children, the one-man band was the eighth wonder of the world. He played drum, cymbals, bells, pipes, triangle and concertina all at once whilst his companion, with the monkey in a brightly coloured fez, marched gaily up and down the street taking round the collecting box.

148 An exotic country spectacle was the travelling bear, here seen outside an Oxfordshire inn, c. 1900. The entertainment was announced by a blast on the bugle, and the bear, chained to his master, invariably a Russian or Pole, would dance and catch the stick when it was thrown to him. Man and beast slept in any barn or shed available to them.

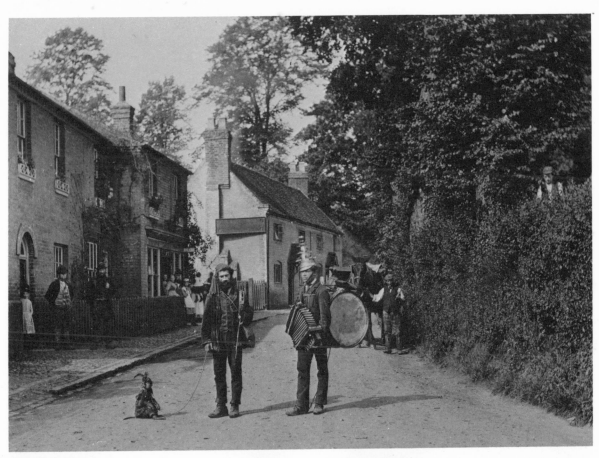

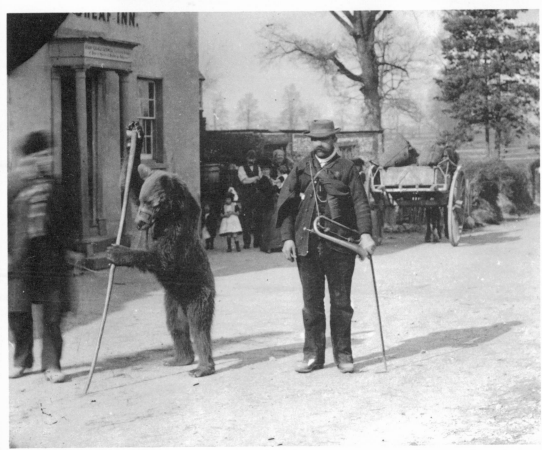

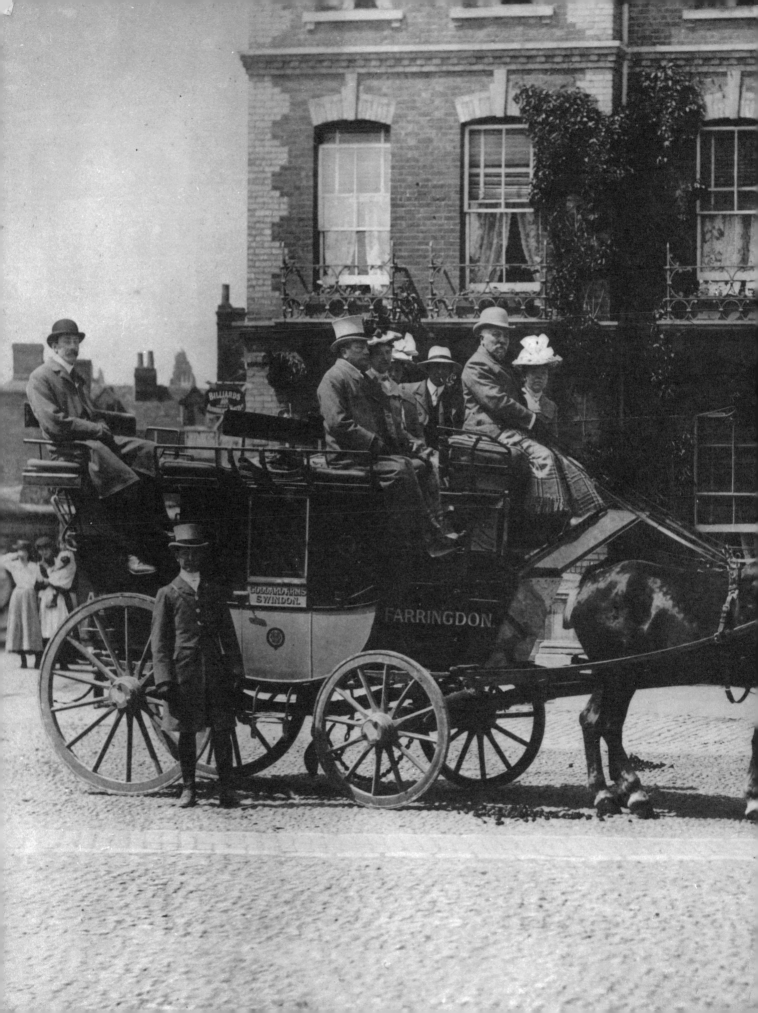

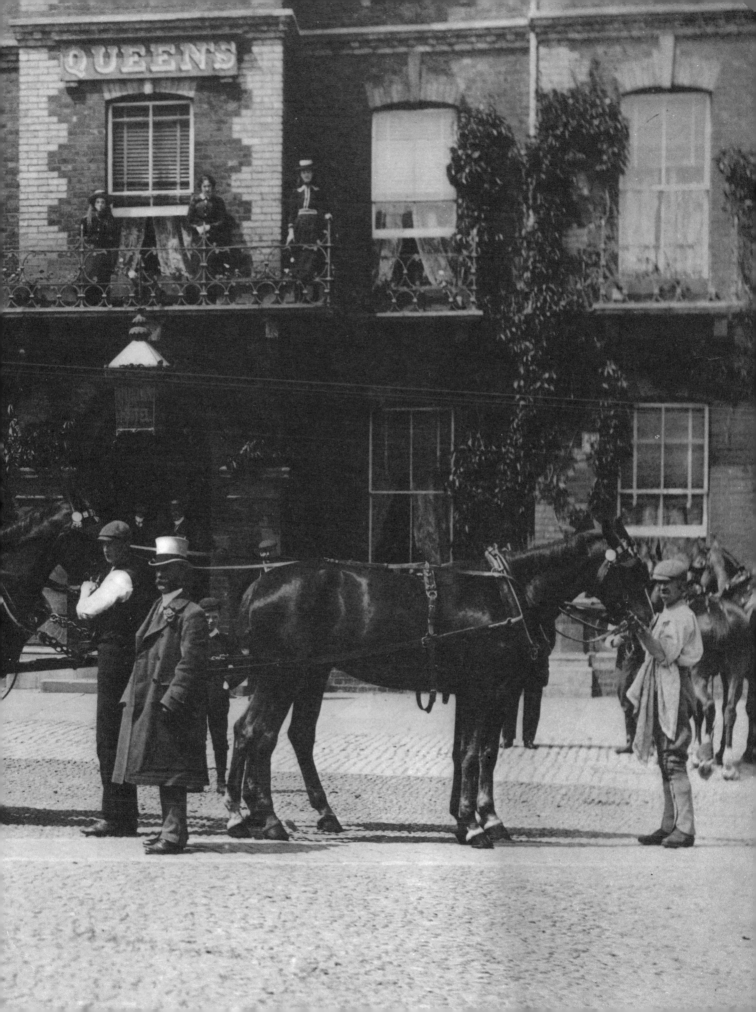

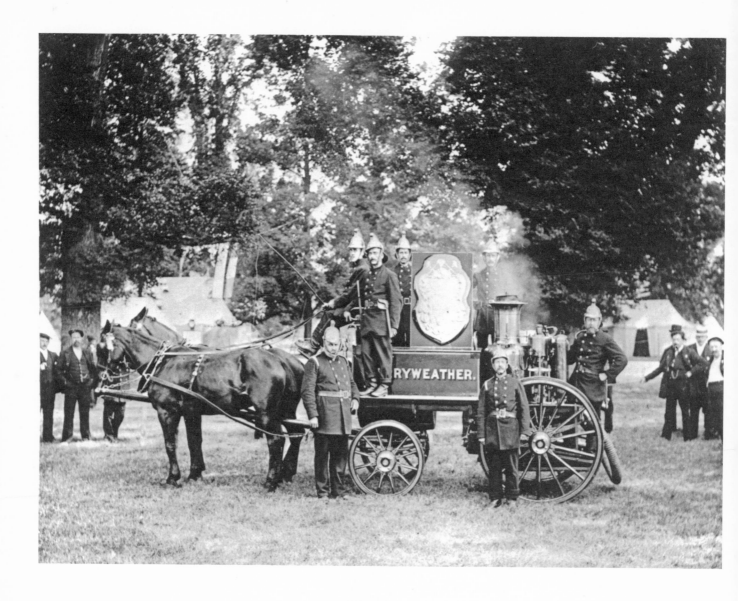

149 *previous page*   This special coaching party, with
coach and four, is a good illustration of wealthy Victorian
society at leisure. Destined for Faringdon, they are
photographed outside the Queen's Hotel, Abingdon,
c. 1885. The building is now largely demolished.

150   A Fire Brigade camp and review held in August
1898 at Blenheim Park, Woodstock. This photograph
shows the Leyton Brigade, proud winners of the Steamer
Shield, with a Merryweather 'Greenwich Gem' Steamer.

151   Taunt has ably captured the elegance of this
Edwardian town carriage or landaulette, probably made
by the New Engine Company of Acton in 1906.

152   The inventive genius of the last century is typified
by Taunt's photograph of an amphibious boat at
Cricklade, Wiltshire, *c.* 1870. The craft was devised to
navigate the shallows of the upper Thames and could also
travel on land.

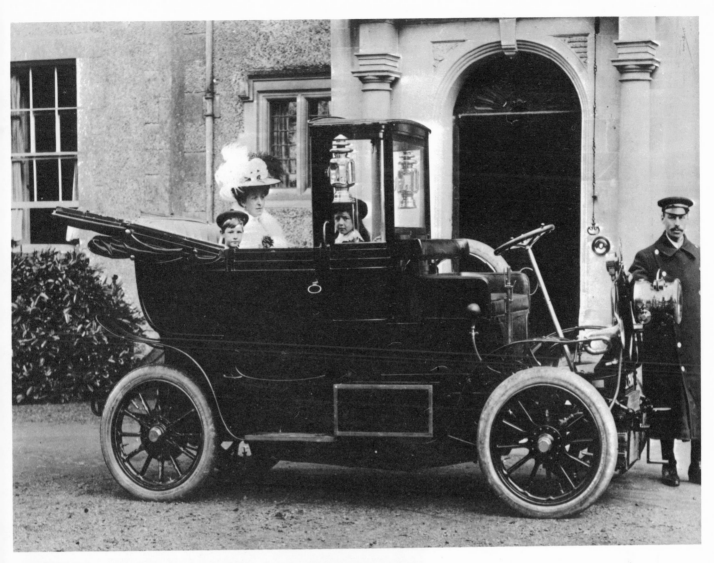

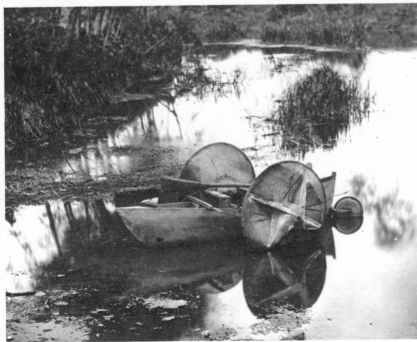

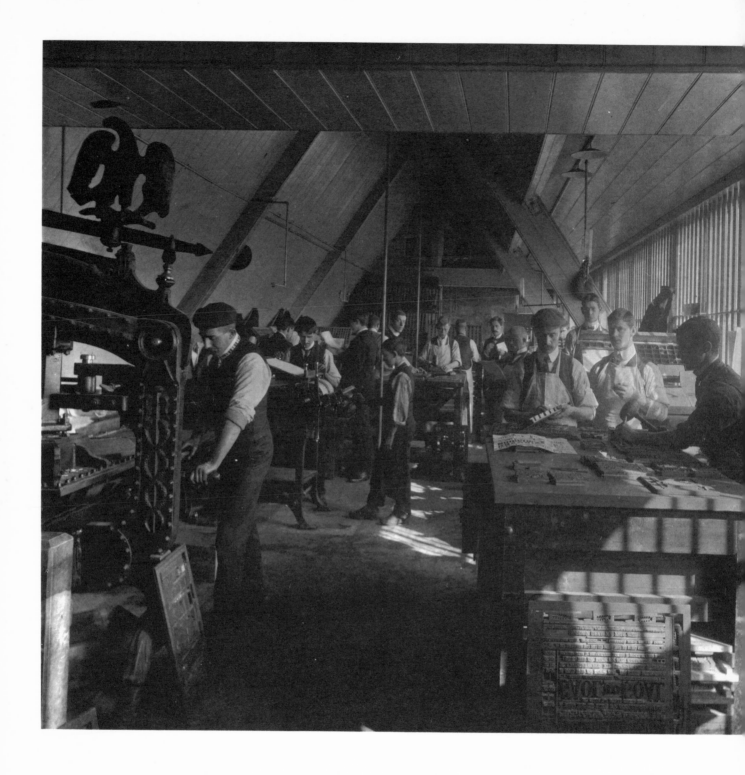

153   The printing works of the Church Army Press in
Cowley, Oxford, *c.* 1905.

154   Workmen grinding the clay, an important process
in canal building near Siddington, Gloucestershire, for
the reconstruction of part of the Thames & Severn
canal, September 1904. The clay in this state is used for
'puddling', a method of building up a firm bank of clay.

155   Roadmakers replacing kidney stones outside Henry
Taunt's Broad Street shop in 1881.

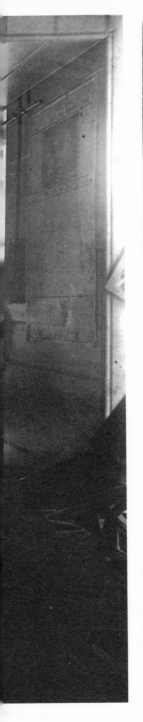
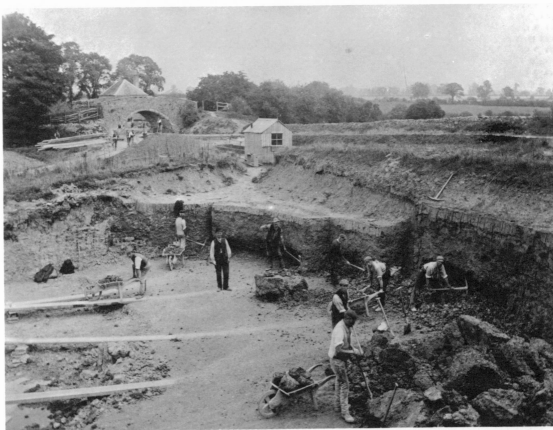
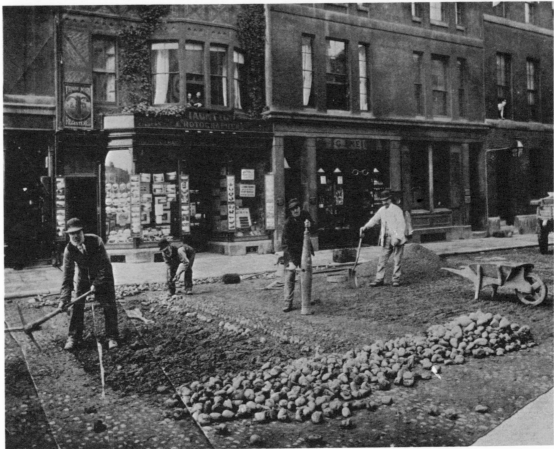

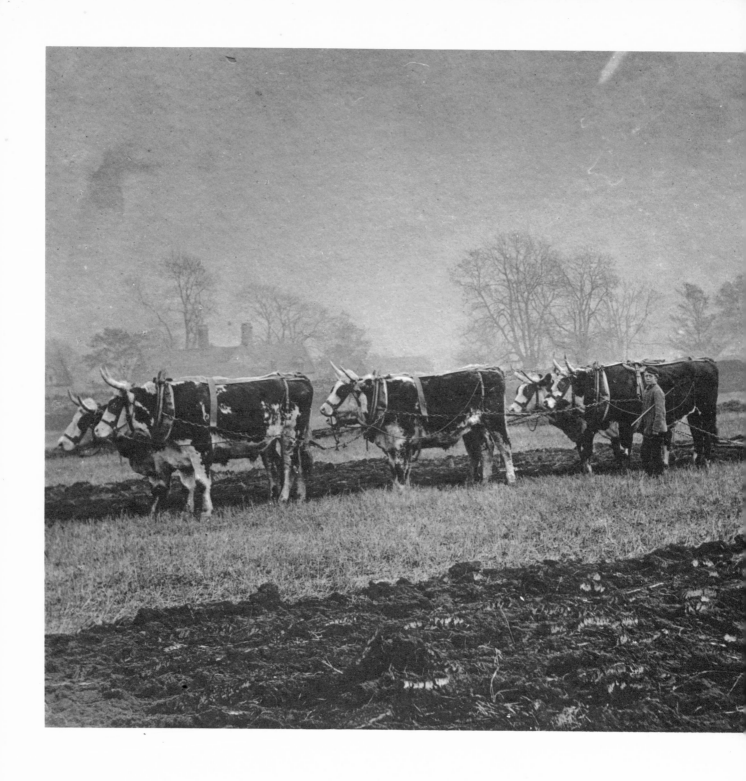

156　A beautiful photograph of six oxen ploughing near the River Windrush in the Cotswolds, *c.* 1895.

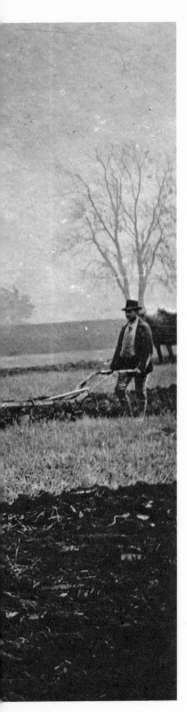

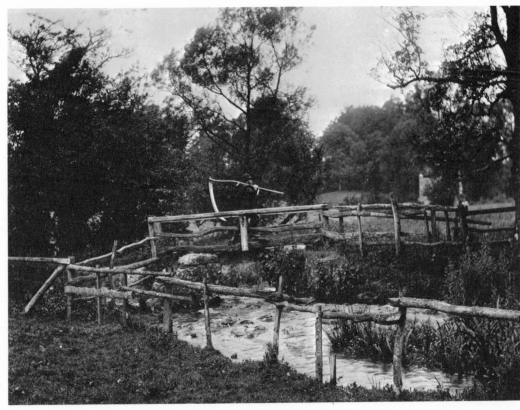

157   A mower carrying his scythe home at the end of the day at Lower Guiting by the Windrush, *c.* 1895.

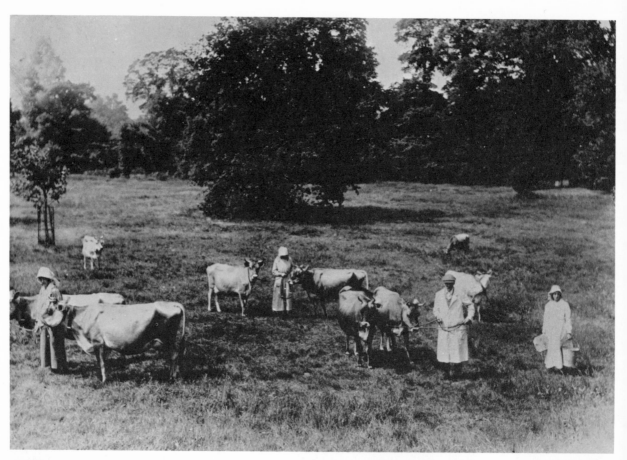

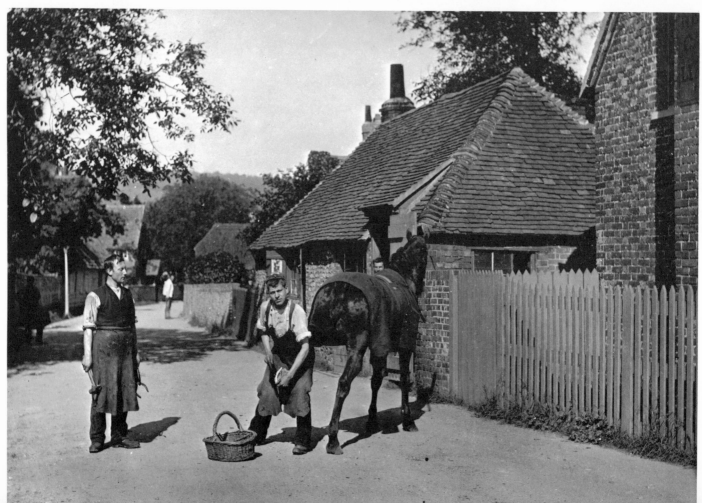

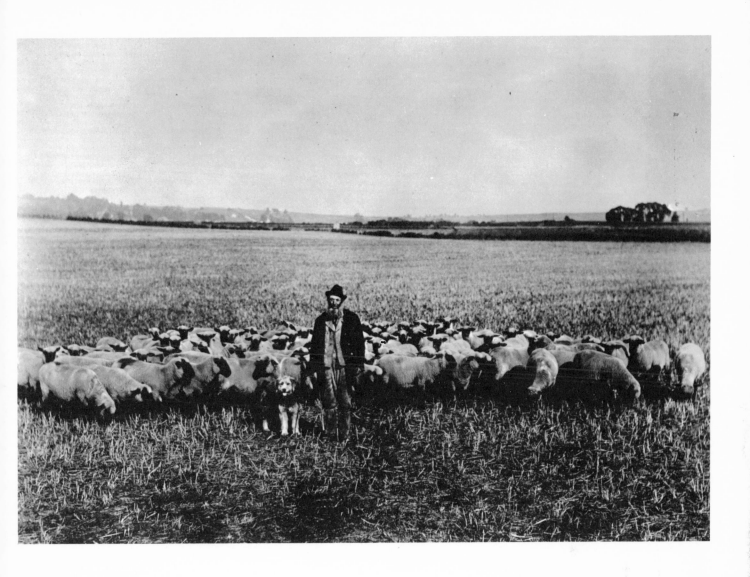

158 The Jersey herd in the grounds of Headington Hill Hall, the home of the Morrells. One of the milk maids is set for work with her pail and stool. It was common-place to take the pail to the cow rather than the cow to the milk shed.

159 A village blacksmith shoeing a horse, *c.* 1885. This is going on outside the smithy, probably to afford Taunt a better light for his photograph. The smith's job was a vital task in an era when communication and agriculture depended largely on the horse.

Myself, my family, my generation, were born in a world of silence; a world of hard work and necessary patience, of backs bent to the ground, hands massaging the crops, of waiting on weather and growth; of villages like ships in the empty landscapes and the long walking distances between them; of white narrow roads, rutted by hooves and cart-wheels, innocent of oil and petrol, down which people passed rarely, and almost never for pleasure, and the horse was the fastest thing moving. Man and horse were all the power we had – abetted by levers and pulleys. But the horse was king, and almost everything grew around him: fodder, smithies, stables, paddocks, distances and the rhythm of our days. His eight miles an hour was the limit of our movements, as it had been since the days of the Romans. That eight miles an hour was life and death, the size of our world, our prison.

Laurie Lee, *Cider with Rosie*, 1959

160 A shepherd with his flock and faithful sheepdog, near the Oxfordshire village of Horsepath around the turn of the century.

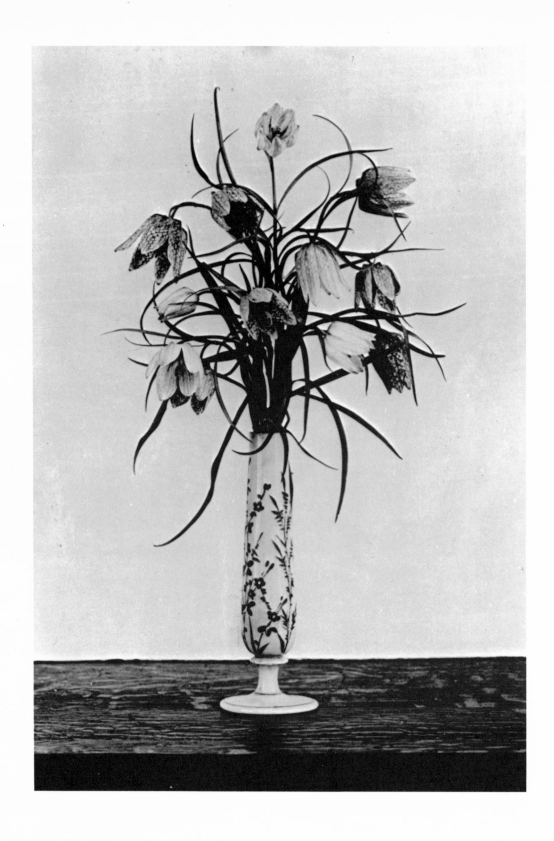

161   White and purple fritillaries, a common-place wild flower around Oxford in the last century, now becoming rare.

Taunt's Ephemera

Most of Henry Taunt's printing activity took place after 1889 when he removed his equipment to the works at 'Rivera' in Cowley. Here he produced not only his books and postcards but a multitude of leaflets, posters, advertisements and 'dainties', as he called them.

What a typical Victorian typographer's sense he had. Every line must be different! Indeed, what a curious collection of typefaces he possessed. These were set to his designs, if that is the correct term; and one can only pity the compositors who had to cope with the intricate setting of type, ornaments and spacing material involved in these designs.

As a designer myself, I find the quaintness of his style a sheer delight. His maps and some of his designs are resolved with a particular sensitivity for the printed page; while those that are not are a constant source of amusement. His symbol is a splendid recognition element and his fluency and directness as a copywriter leave little to be desired. I for one find great joy in this work of Taunt's.

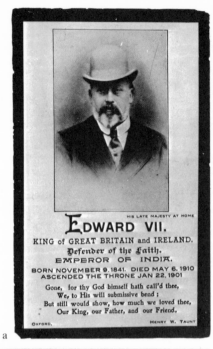

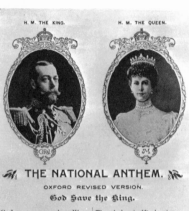

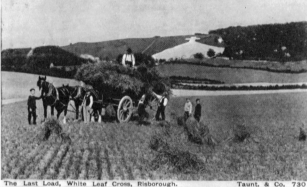

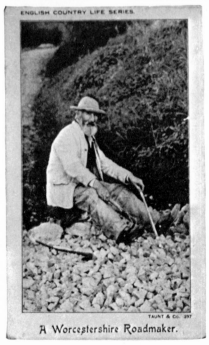

a

b

c

d

e

162 [a, b, c, d, e] A selection of postcards from his many series. The photographic picture-postcard was introduced in this country by the Rotary Photographic Company in 1900.

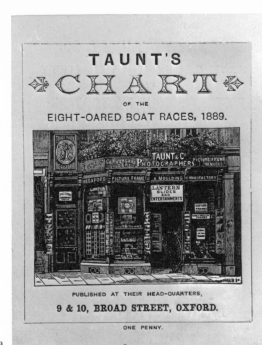

a

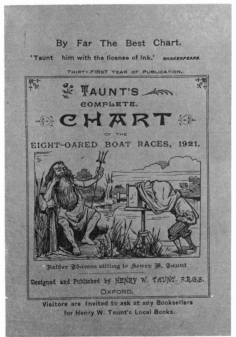

b

c

Father Thames sitting to H. W. Taunt for his Photograph.

Old Father Thames.

—o—

1.

OLD Father Thames, one lovely day, reclined to take his ease;
The sun shone bright with glorious light, and softened was the breeze;
And ripples small, laughed each and all, as on they speeded by;
And many a bird, in song was heard, while soaring in the sky.

**You are respectfully invited to visit Taunt's House-Boat
at the Red Post during the Races.**

2.

Old Father Thames enjoyed his nap, as people often do,
And woke refresh'd from perfect rest, in a good humour too;
Said to himself—" amid my wealth, one thing alone I want
Some pictures bright, in this fair light, at once I'll send for Taunt."

3.

" Yes! Taunt's the man, if any can, he always does things well ;
He's wrought for me, for years thirty, I'm very glad to tell
His last new Guide is quite my pride, he seems to know my thought,
And writes it down, to my renown, in language wanting naught."

4.

" I peep like mouse into his house, which floats upon my stream,
And note him still, combining skill with perfect Artist's theme.
A visit pay him any day, Taunt welcomes one and all,
And shows them o'er his treasure store, if they will only call."

5.

" I always see him like a bee, at work with all his pow'r,
Chaining the dancing sunbeams, which play with every hour,
And pretty scenes, round village greens, he often steals for me:
Scenes dull or bright, and day or night, and valley glen, or lea. "

6.

" You'll find Taunt's boat each day afloat, close by the old red post,
Near Cherwell's tide, whose silent glide within my bosom's lost.
Now do your best with earnest zest, to help him on his way ;
Buy all you want from my friend Taunt, and don't forget to pay."

**Taunt's Photographs of Oxford and his River Scenes
are far the Best.**

---

163   Taunt began publishing his Charts of the Oxford University Boat Race in 1881 and they were continued annually until after his death. [a] The cover of the 1889 Chart features Swain's wood-cut illustration of the Broad Street shop. [b] The cover of the 1921 Chart shows Ferrier's drawing of Father Thames and H. W. Taunt, which is supplemented by [c] a spread from the Chart of 1892 with one of Taunt's delightful poems. Incidentally, he seldom missed a chance of advertising his other publications, as the last line shows.

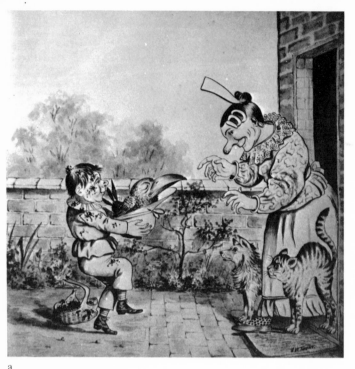

a

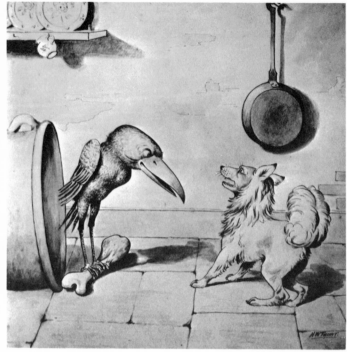

b

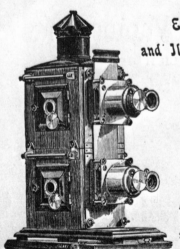

a

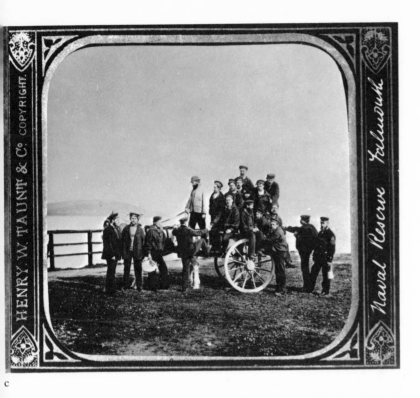

c

Revival of Mr. Henry W. Taunt's Popular Children's Party.

One thousand Oxford Lads and Lassies

are cordially invited to the

CORN EXCHANGE, OXFORD.

ON

Wednesday, December 19th, 1906.

AT 5. IN THE AFTERNOON.

TO

Mr. Henry W. Taunt's,

Children's Party,

Two hours glorious ENTERTAINMENT and FUN
Scenes, CINEMATOGRAPH, Fairy & Humorous Stories,
with Music &c.

Mr. Taunt has been asked so many times, 'Why don't you give us some of those most delightful Children's Parties, you gave for many years in the old Town Hall,' that he has now decided to do so, and cordially invites all his older friends who used to enjoy themselves, to bring THEIR Children and give THEM a Treat.

Don't forget. Wednesday December 19th at 5 p.m.

Front Seats, Reserved. One Shilling.   Back Seats, Sixpence.

Doors open at 5. Commence at 5.30. Carriages for 7.30.

For Programme see next page.

b

164   Two illustrations from a lantern slide series devised, written and drawn by Taunt. It is called 'Hookey beak the Raven – That Raven wasn't good'. These are the captions from the readings:
[a] 'And you shall be my raven, with me shall allus stay, And Aunt Matilda Tabitha shall feed you everyday.'

[b] 'Now Hookey beak the Raven to his earthen pan has flown,
For like the Welshman Taffy, he'd stolen a marrow bone.
The bone belongs to Tootsicon, who was a little pup.
Says Tootsicon to Hookey beak, "Now just you give that up."
But Hookey beak he wouldn't, he looked as though he'd fight!'

[c] An early photographic lantern slide taken at Falmouth, c. 1870.

165   Two of Taunt's advertisements for his entertainments, [a] showing a lantern similar to the one he used and [b] publicizing a children's party of 1906.

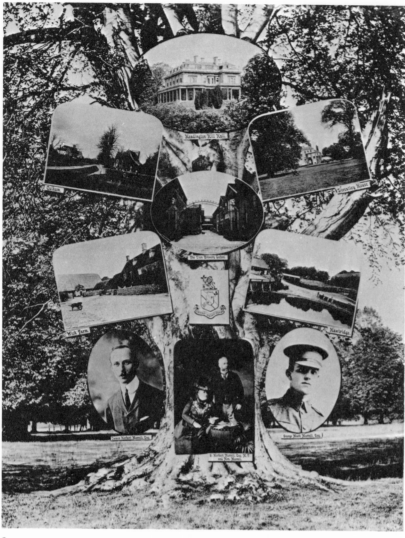

a

b

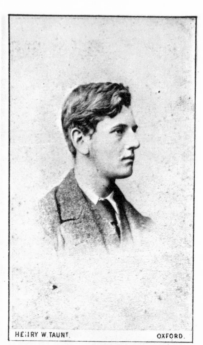

HENRY W. TAUNT   OXFORD.

Photographer to the Oxford Architectural Society

VIEWS OF
OXFORD
& THE NEIGHBOURHOOD
ALSO
THE THAMES & ITS TOWNS
FROM ITS SOURCE TO LONDON BRIDGE

PHOTOGRAPHED BY

Henry W. Taunt

10, Broad Str?
& 33, Corn Market Str?
OXFORD.

Portraits in every style from
Cartes de visite to life size

N? 4894

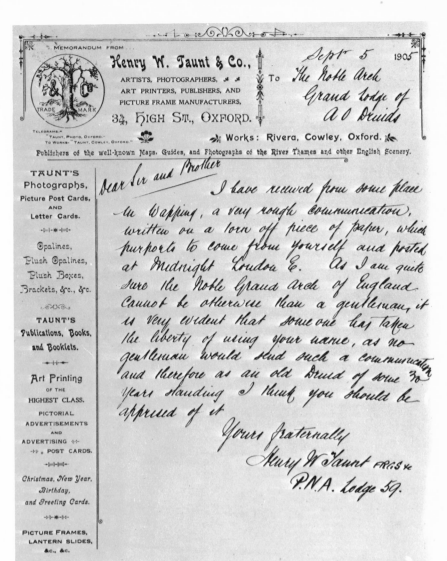

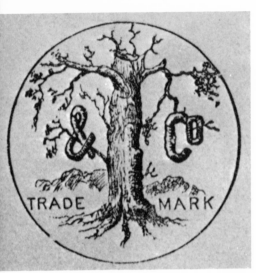

166 Photographic Ephemera.
[a] A photograph pictorializing the Morrell family tree.
[b] A *carte-de-visite* of an unknown man. These portraits were originally intended as visiting cards but became items collected for the family album. They were at the height of their popularity in the 1860s and 1870s. On the back of the *carte* the photographer would advertise his business. Here we see the fine flourish of Taunt's own hand.

167 [a] Taunt's trademark which appears on most of his work. He explains, 'This our trade mark, signifies Progress, Novel Ideas and Good Work'.
[b] An application to his letterhead.

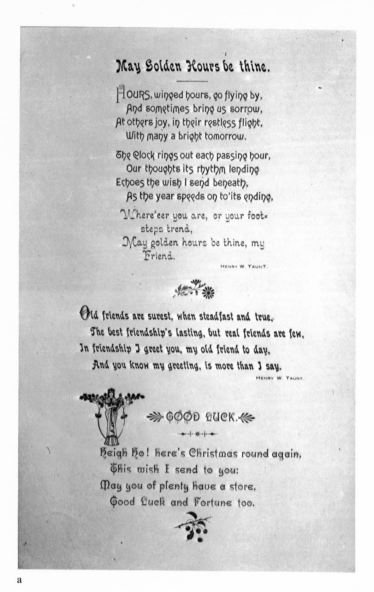

a

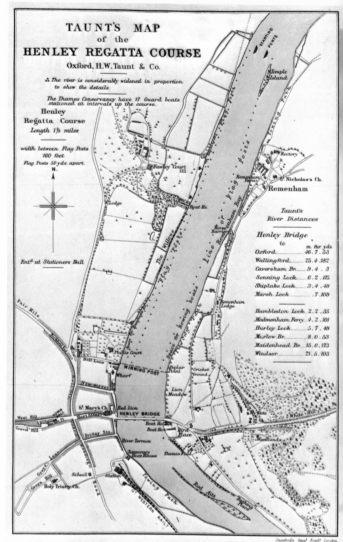

b

168 Two examples of Taunt's typographic and map work. [a] A page of a booklet advertising his Christmas and New Year Cards, 1903–4, with his own poems, and [b] a map of the Henley Regatta Course, 1886.

169 Ephemera of the 1914–18 war. Words and music of a recruiting song written and composed by Taunt. The proceeds from sales went to a local war charity.

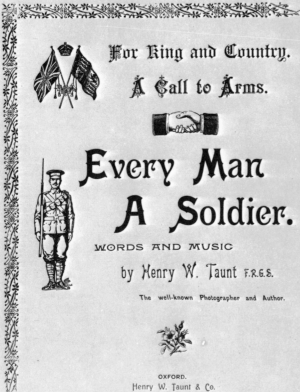

For King and Country.

A Call to Arms.

Every Man A Soldier.

WORDS AND MUSIC

by Henry W. Taunt F.R.G.S.

The well-known Photographer and Author.

OXFORD.

Henry W. Taunt & Co.

SOLD FOR THE OXFORD WAR FUND.

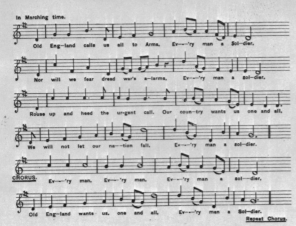

Every Man A Soldier.

New Patriotic Song by Henry W. Taunt.

In Marching time.

Old Eng—land calls us all to Arms, Ev—'ry man a Sol—dier,

Nor will we fear dread war's a—larms, Ev—'ry man a sol—dier.

Rouse up and heed the ur—gent call. Our coun—try wants us one and all,

We will not let our na—tion fall. Ev—'ry man a sol—dier.

CHORUS. Ev—'ry man, Ev—'ry man, Ev—'ry man a sol—dier,

Old Eng—land wants us, one and all, Ev—'ry man a Sol—dier.

Repeat Chorus.

Every man a Soldier.

New Patriotic Song.

Old England calls us all to Arms,
　　Every man a soldier,
Nor will we fear dread war's alarms,
　　Every man a soldier,
Rouse up and heed the urgent call,
Our country wants us, one and all,
We will not let our nation fall,
　　Every man a soldier.

Chorus.　Every man, every man,
　　　　Every man a soldier,
　　Old England wants us one and all,
　　　　Every man a soldier.

Shall we refrain and let her go?
　　Every man a soldier,
What play the Coward? No! No! No!
　　Every man a soldier,
We'll not stand by with folded hands,
While Germans ravish home and lands,
And make us slaves with their demands,
　　Every man a soldier.

Chorus.　Every man, every man,
　　　　Every man a soldier,
　　Old England calls us, that's enough,
　　　　Every man a soldier.

And when at last the victory's won,
　　Every man a soldier
We'll glory in the work well done,
　　Every man a soldier,
Ah! then shall follow sweet release.
For wars shall end and tumults cease,
A THOUSAND YEARS of GLORIOUS PEACE!
　　Now, Every man a soldier.

Chorus.　Every man, Every man,
　　　　Every man a soldier,
　　We battle now to win the right,
　　　　Every man a soldier.

Henry W. Taunt

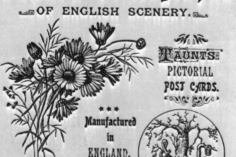
170 Two of Taunt's advertisements: [a] to promote his
photographs, [b] for his printing services. [c] Taunt's
political poster for the Oxford local elections of 1908.

Afterword

My personal involvement with Taunt's work began when I was writing a history of Iffley, a village near Oxford, and looking for some material to illustrate the local customs. I found Taunt's photographs and they answered my problem perfectly. Consequently I became completely enchanted by his work and the more I discovered, the more I wanted to know. The story of his life and times gradually fell into place, and for me it seemed to typify the nineteenth century I would have known had I been born a hundred years earlier, the Oxford of a local person. In fact, pleasingly, our Oxfords frequently correspond.

I was born and spent most of my childhood in Cowley not a mile from 'Rivera'. I frequently played in the Marsh Brook at Mud Lane as the children in Plate 127, and can clearly visualize a chance meeting with the old man in the places with which I was so familiar. 'Skinners' Pool' was a name that baffled my youthful thoughts during the frequent Thames fishing outings of my early teens, and I was delighted to discover Taunt's story of the area and the people who lived there. My father worked for twenty years at the Church Army Press in Temple Road, Cowley, and in many ways my vague recollections of the place are not so different from Plate 153. I have also reproduced one of the Iffley pictures, and to complete the association, the young girl who was the May Queen in 1906 (Plate 141) was my wife's great aunt Phyllis.

It is fifty years since Taunt died. Much has happened to our native Oxford, much at which Taunt would be aghast. The University and its splendid medieval buildings remain intact and probably always will. But it is our Oxford, the Oxford that was St Ebbe's, the Oxford of St Clement's and Jericho, domestic Victorian Oxford that is so ruthlessly disappearing. In putting together this selection of Taunt's photographs, it is my hope that the remaining joys of the city and the surrounding countryside will still exist in another fifty years for the benefit of a future generation.

Oxford   B.W.B.

Acknowledgments and Pictorial Sources

I would like to express my sincere thanks to the following individuals and authorities for their help in compiling and illustrating this book:

First to my wife, Buzz, who has withstood many months of domestic upheaval and without her help and encouragement I would not have completed this work; Mr Kingsley Belsten, for his considerable help throughout the period of my research and subsequently reading through my manuscript and making many valuable suggestions; the late Miss Mary Nichols, of the Oxford City Reference Library, who spent many hours searching and plying me with information from her intimate knowledge of local history, her recent death is a sad loss to Oxford; Mr J. P. Wells, the Oxford City Librarian; Mr Malcolm Graham and the staff of the Oxford City Reference Library; Mr R. R. Bolland of the Thames Conservancy who gave me much valuable information from his sound knowledge of the Thames; Mr David Francis for his advice with regard to the magic lantern and its use in entertainment; Mr Nicolas Cooper and other staff at the National Monuments Record; Mr David Vaisey of the Bodleian Library, Oxford; the Royal Geographical Society; the Royal Photographic Society; the City of Oxford Motor Services; the *Oxford Mail and Times*; the late Mr Edward Cordrey; Mrs Linda Herring; Mr W. A. Adams; Mr F. W. Benham; Sir Basil Blackwell; Mr Gordon Winter, Chief Assistant Editor of *Country Life*; Dr David Thomas of the Science Museum, Kensington; Mr Jasper Scovil of Magdalen College, Oxford; and Mr Alan Turner of Turner Gee Studios who copied many of the photographs. I further tender my thanks to many other individuals, librarians and archivists whose libraries and institutions I visited and with whom I corresponded. Unfortunately their numbers render it impossible for me to list them all by name.

I am indebted to the following by whose kind permission the photographs and other material have been made available: Bodleian Library, Oxford 78, 162d, 163c, 168a; British Museum 4-6, 168b; Buckinghamshire County Museum 35; Mr David Francis 164c, 166b; Howarth-Loomes Collection 44, 55; The President and Fellows of Magdalen College, Oxford 59, 62, 71, 72, 77; National Monuments Record 2, 11, 12, 15, 16, 22, 25-6, 36-7, 40-1, 45-6, 50-1, 54, 56-8, 69, 79-81, 83, 85-7, 91, 94-5, 98, 106, 112-16, 120, 123-4, 127, 135, 142-3, 145-9, 151-3, 156-7, 159; Oxford City Library 3, 7, 13, 19, 21, 23-4, 27-9, 32-4, 39, 60-1, 64-8, 70, 73-6, 82, 84, 88-90, 92-3, 97, 101-5, 108-10, 117-19, 125-6, 128-31, 137-8, 140-1, 150; 154-5, 158, 160-1, 162a, 163a, b, 164a, b, 165b, 166a, 167b, 169, 170b, c; Thames Conservancy 9, 14, 17-18, 49, 122.

Illustrations not included in this list are from the author's own collection. The photographs from the National Monuments Record are reproduced by kind permission of the Oxford City Library Committee.